9781737990512

AF134402

Pir
Vilayat
Inayat
Khan

Do you remember
    Having existed long before the birth of your body
        before your body was fashioned out of the fabric of the planet earth
So that you were able to smell the earth and breathe the air, and
    listen to the rumble of the thunder
        and pass your glance across the darkness
            and reach the face of the stars?

Do you remember the landscapes of the worlds of the soul?
Do you remember the choirs?
        Do you remember the symphonies of the spheres?
Do you remember the celebrations?
Do you remember the processions of legions of beings—heralds,
            angels, archangels—beings of all kinds
      converging upon a throne made of glory rather than of gold?
And do you remember the emotion of jubilation. . . .
    The great celebrations?

    Surely you must remember something of this . . .

Do you remember having been a cosmic being . . .
nameless . . . formless . . . ethereal . . .
made out of the substance of pure light?
Do you remember having been kindled like a candle . . .
just as light passes from one candle to another . . .
Do you remember the emotion that you experienced when coming in contact
with wonderful Beings?
Do you remember the Masters?   The Saints?   The Prophets?
Do you remember the Archangels and the Angels?
Do you remember all the festivities out of which you were born –
of which you are a part?

This is the meaning of the cosmic celebration in the heavens . . . . . .

. . . And this is the inspiration

for the Music
from the Hearts
of Space.

In all earlier world cultures music stood at the service of ritual, of the holy cult, of consciousness-expansion and the deepest in human experience. The intuitive understanding of this significance would be a precondition for a new auditory consciousness, capable of being applied to all today's varieties of music—whether Classical, Pop, Jazz, Avant-garde. . . . It is precisely through the energies of such musical works that we may discover within ourselves the road that leads to the regions of the soul and spirit.

Peter Michael Hamel

What we call music . . . is only a miniature, which our intelligence has grasped from that music or harmony of the whole universe which is working behind everything, and which is the source and origin of nature. It is because of this that the wise of all ages have considered music to be a sacred art.

Hazrat Inayat Khan

THE HEARTS OF SPACE GUIDE

To Cosmic, Transcendent and Innerspace Music

An annotated listing
of the music heard since 1973
on the weekly radio program
Music from the Hearts of Space

by

Stephen Hill & Anna Turner

Graphic design by Janaia Marisolle

Passion of an instant
Births all eternity
Space illuminates
Depth's darkness
Infinity breathes
The worlds of universe
Ringing sounds
Envelop silence

Alexander Scriabin

ACKNOWLEDGMENTS

The following people have made direct contributions to the publication of this book. We acknowledge them with deepest appreciation and love: Dan Dugan, Hokulea Parrish, Nina Ireland, Stephen Coughlin, Leni Mayer, Michael Toms.

And also…
The incredible heartforce of space explorers who listen to **Music from the Hearts of Space** and have communicated with us over the years. Your energies have contributed directly to this taking form.

The musicians…and the wise beings who have inspired us with their understandings of music, and whose words we quote.

And especially Janaia Marisolle, graphic designer, who understood—everything—on every level, and added dimensions to our understanding. She has been the third energy that transformed this project of two people into a whole.

Dedicated to
The Hearts Devas

TABLE OF CONTENTS

THE SOUND EXPERIENCE OF "MUSIC FROM THE HEARTS OF SPACE"

All things and beings in the universe
are connected with each other, visibly and invisibly,
and through vibrations a communication is established between them
on all planes of existence.

Hazrat Inayat Khan

Music from the Hearts of Space with Timitheo and Anna is broadcast every Sunday night on Berkeley's KPFA-FM, from 11 p.m. to 2 a.m. It's a time of minimum ambient noise, when the psychic scatter over the Bay Area is quieted and something of a subtler nature can move in the atmospheres. The music we play we call ancient and contemporary transcendent music, inner and outer space music. It's music that opens . . . . allows . . . . creates space.

We tune to the vibratory space of a particular night and improvise with it—live—sometimes blending into it, gliding in it, sometimes counterpointing (once in a while missing it completely . . . lost in space). Each night is different. We have deep space, crystal space, high space, almost clear nights, crescent moons, dreamy nights, uncertain nights, nights flying in the friendly skies. It is an exquisite attunement, reading the nights, deepening into them—and a practice of alignment-in-fluidity to work in them.

Some people have wanted to call Hearts of Space "new age." We think of it as universal. It seems unproductive to label some kinds of music good and some bad, or 'higher,' 'lower,' more 'evolved' or more 'spiritual.' The magnificent pulse of life rushes and breaks over and through us when we dance; the ecstasy of drums brings deep connection. Music speaks of life, and life is spiritual.

We do love and play a particular kind of music, one that, for us, creates space for deep, immeasurable journeys. Rather, it creates a way to enter a space that is always there, as close as the heart, a slightly different frequency . . . a breath away. We enter the space by allowing it to enter us. In that expansion we can all go as far as we wish, propelled by our infinite inner possibilities, influenced by the coordinates of the psychic moment, restricted only by where we think we can arrive.

Certain pieces do suggest certain directions. There are sounds of other dimensions, brought back and transmuted into earth frequencies, resonating energy templates to bring forth certain states; sound holograms that can be changed or stretched or colored in the hearing. Aural fragrances, radiant liquid pools of sound, shimmering and pulsing, crystal essences that seem like seeds of vast galactic swirls of hidden music. There are those rare, ecstatic works that reach into the ineffable, taking us beyond ourselves and through ourselves, in which we seem to melt. Some of the music bathes the heart softly. Some brings us into remembrance. And if, in those moments, time's illusion bends, every-thing expands. Each piece, each time, is different. There is no end to it all. . . .

There are other commonalities. The music we play is based in harmony. Sounds which are harmonic with one another give a sense of completion and completeness. Dissonance, like the existential pessimism it has often companioned, seems always to be seeking resolution. The listener may be led to find and provide it, but that is another kind of journey.

Our late night music is rarely sharply percussive, and if brass instrumentation ap-pears in Hearts of Space journeys, it is usually softened—muted or electronically proc-essed. Synthesizers can sustain a note timelessly and build great heavenly ascents of it. Strings and voices have those capabilities naturally; passed through electronics they reach toward the sounds we remember with our expanded memories.

If you truly surrender to music, particularly this music, it will take you somewhere. Our normal listening is distant, analytical, objective. We're looking for information—comparing, judging. With space music and ambient sound we slide through the audible barrier and immerse ourselves in sound. We listen to the entire field around us, and it affects our entire field.

Music generates energy. It has as great an effect on the subtler levels of our organisms as food does on the physical. Obviously, cayenne and sushi and chocolate cake and pears generate different energies, adjust and change our bodies and psyches with their particular electrochemistries. Different musics, too, alter our emotional fields with their refined, electromagnetic energies. What we decide to consume and energize ourselves with is a moment-to-moment choice.

What we do on Music from the Hearts of Space is to choose a piece to begin the program, that feels like the night—usually reflective of it, though sometimes a harmonic and sometimes another note entirely that makes a chord with it. And then we move—as it moves—staying on the edge of the moment, listening . . . waiting . . . responding . . . initiating. . . .

The music contained in these pages are the notes we play with. We wish you beautiful, unexpected, elegant high flights.

With love,

Anna Turner

Night opens wide
The gates of space,
Makes of the earth
A flying star,
On which we travel
Through the All
Like arrows, speeding
To an unknown aim.

The magic orb
Moves ceaselessly
Through unknown realms.
From where? Where to?
It carries us
From void to void
Through time—and
Through eternity.

And thus we move
Within the space
Of our mind-created All,
From dream to dream,
From orb to orb,
Until the void within us
Can absorb—the Light
That is both origin and aim.

Lama Anagarika Govinda

THE RADIO PROGRAM "MUSIC FROM THE HEARTS OF SPACE"

The name came in on a sunny fall day in 1972 during a meditation in my backyard in San Francisco. I heard it clearly and wrote it down. At the time, we were applying to KPFA to do a new series of radio programs and needed a name. I felt the one I received was a gift, and now, after living with it for eight years, I understand it as the code name/mantram of our planetary space mission (We chose to accept it . . .).

The music which has found its way into our collection—some through obvious, some through obscure, means—has amplified and deepened the original concept in ways I never could have imagined. Our simple, unconscious yearnings for a music of sensitivity and depth have evolved into the multidimensional assortment we present to you in this catalogue. Throughout our explorations, the concept **Music from the Hearts of Space** has been a guide, a touchstone, an inspiration. . . .

Today our incessant exposure to any and all of the music ever created has resulted in a new condition: music has become a psychological necessity. At the same time, the bewildering variety of choices creates confusion and the need for special guides. For, lying just beneath the ubiquitous pulse of the popular music of the day, the sensitive, deepening core of us all REQUIRES regular contact with a music capable of serving as a medium for psychological growth, inner healing and communion. This is why a listener writes to us: "Your music is just essential. . . ."

We have accepted the idea that **all music is spiritual** in the broad sense, but some music is more able to serve as "a form of spatial food for our finer being bodies." It is this music we seek to discover (or rediscover) and transmit to the growing number of contemporary listeners who are ready to use it.

This catalogue is not even complete, let alone definitive. However, it represents the best beginning we are capable of making toward the service of helping aware listeners find the psychic food needed for their journey. We are anticipating that the years to come will bring the opportunity to expand and deepen the scope of the listings. For now please accept this guide in its infant state, with understanding. It will lead you to the high regions of the heart. . . .

Love on your Journeys,

Stephen Hill
(Timitheo)

Universal music
opening space
to fluid realms

Starstreams
of deep harmonies
connecting
Endless chords
Turning
in
the renewing vastness of heart

Music of peace
and self-absorption
The sounds of distance
and center
of earth magic
and Remembrance

HOW TO USE THIS GUIDE

*The Great Way is not difficult
for those who have no preferences...
Make the smallest distinction, however,
And heaven and earth are set infinitely apart...*

Senstan, Third Chinese Patriarch of Zen

God help us, this music list is divided into categories. We arrived at these distinctions through a combination of insight and necessity. We can only hope that they will serve you as they have served us, as a mental organizing tool. Think of them as flexible, organic containers. Within each category the selections are listed **roughly** in order of frequency of airplay over the last four years. RELATED MUSIC listings are pieces which we play only occasionally, and include without comment as being valuable and worth checking out if you have the opportunity. Again, this is a library of music played in the late-night hours; it is not intended to be an inclusive list of spiritual music.

THE LISTINGS: TABLE OF CONTENTS

CONTEMPORARY ANCIENT

Music made today with awareness of the sounds and expressions of the deep past.

HALEAKALA

Chaitanya Hari Deuter
Kuckuck 2375-042

Haleakala Mystery, Just for This Moment, Crystal Pearls Crystal, Mein Geliebter berührt mich, umarmt mich der Wind

One of the finest albums of contemporary eastern influenced meditation music. Haleakala Mystery is one of the most magically evocative pieces we have.

GYMNOSPHERE: SONG OF THE ROSE

Jordan de la Sierra
Unity Records UR-701

entire album

Double or single album. Improvised musical meditations for harmonically tuned, spatially expanded piano. Deep, lyrical and ancient as Babylon. Reverberation recorded in Grace Cathedral.

SUNBORNE

Constance Demby
Gandharva Performing Arts Co., 225 Tamalpais Rd., Fairfax, CA 94930 (cassette)

Darkness of Space, The Dawning, One With the Light

Deep interior tunings and calls of returning to places unremembered . . . many, many thousands of years . . . but not totally forgotten. Extraordinary sounds.

ECSTASY

Chaitanya Hari Deuter
Kuckuck 044

Ecstasy, Back to a Planet, Night Rain, Blue Waves Gold

A superlative work that seems to reflect the deep joy, inner peace and musical love of its composer. Produced in Deuter's 4-track studio in the Rajneesh ashram in Poona, India.

O'CEAN

Larkin
Wind Sung Sounds, 1259 El Camino Real, Suite 9, Menlo Park, CA 94025

Emergence

Larkin's flute blended with and inspired by the great whale spirits. Very high vibratory offering.

IN THE GREAT ABBEY OF CLEMENT VI

Stuart Dempster
S-1775
1750 Arch Records, 1750 Arch St., Berkeley, CA 94709

Standing Waves

Trombone improvisations with the 14 second echo space at Pope Clement VI's abbey in Avignon, France.

NIGHT'S CASCADING THREADS OF SPLENDOR

Jordan de la Sierra
unpublished tape

entire work

Our first meeting with the legendary Jordan de la Sierra took place on a full moon night in 1976 when he appeared, unannounced, at the back door of KPFA during Hearts of Space and demanded to play the piano. This improvisation for spacepiano is the result. Excellent music, though not the refined tuning and spatial quality of Song of the Rose, recorded in '77.

MEETINGS WITH REMARKABLE MEN

Thomas de Hartman, Laurence Rosenthal
Varese Sarabande STV 81129

Prince Lubovedsky, The Journey, The Great Prayer

Soundtrack from the Peter Brook film. Fine orchestration and conducting by Laurence Rosenthal of an eclectic mixture of traditional Eastern and Western religious music creates an album worth owning. A+ sound quality.

THE VOICE OF SILENCE

Peter Michael Hamel
Wergo

Panta Tantra, The Voice of Silence

Solo album derived from Indian and Buddhist metaphysical teachings. Creates the experience of ego death as convincingly as one ever need hear it. Also much Indian-derived chanting.

COLOURS OF TIME

Peter Michael Hamel
Kuckuck 046

Colours of Time I and II

1980 album of cyclic type meditative organ/ synthesizer music similar to parts of the earlier Nada. Uncompromised.

HOSIANNA MANTRA

Popol Vuh
Celestial Harmonies 004

entire album

Non-traditional mantra for pure female voice, piano, cembalo, guitar, oboe, tamboura, violin and electronics. The finest of this group's early albums of "sacred" acoustic/electric music.

IMPLOSIONS

Stephan Micus
Japo 60017

Dorenkind, Amarchaj, For the Beautiful Changing Child, For M'schr and Djingis Khan, As I Crossed a Bridge of Dreams

Impeccable original music derived from ancient ethnic musics and played on timeless instruments by a contemporary German artist.

INSIDE

Paul Horn
Epic BXN 26466

entire album

Flute meditations echoing through the exquisite, light space of the Taj Mahal. A classic.

INSIDE THE GREAT PYRAMID

Paul Horn
Mushroom Records MRS-5507

entire album

Double album recorded in the King's and Queen's Chambers of the Great Pyramid of Cheops and the burial chamber at Kephren. Paul Horn chants and uses various flutes tuned to the frequency of the spaces. Darker music than Inside the Taj Mahal.

INSIDE II

Paul Horn
Epic KE 31600

Akasha, Bach Chorales #10, #13, #164, #270

Followup album to Inside. First side is a concept journey through the five elements. Side 2 contains Paul Horn's famous duet with the orca whale, Haida. More musical variety, not as space-creating, but very good.

HARPS OF THE ANCIENT TEMPLES

Gail Laughton
Laurel Record LH-111

entire album

Reissue of a much loved album which was 10 years ahead of its time. Evokes or recreates the harp music of distant times.

LIVING WATERS

Ry Hay
unpublished

entire tape

The experience of resonating with the earth from deep inside a cathedral-sized cistern carved into the island of Ibiza. Ry Hay, suspended on a bosun's chair, chants and sings with the space.

SKIES ABOVE SKIES

Constance Demby
Ghandarva Performing Arts Co., 225 Tamalpais Rd., Fairfax, CA 94930 (cassette)

Om Mani Padme Hum, Peace of God, Sant Ji I Love Thee

Live recording of a concert of devotional song/meditations for space bass, tamboura, harmonium, metal instruments and church echo. Constance Demby's singing creates a powerful presence.

TILL THE END OF TIME

Stephan Micus
Japo 60026

Till the End of Time, For Wis and Ramin

Another of Micus' superb albums of original music played on traditional and contemporary acoustic instruments. Refined and beautiful.

THE VIOLET FLAME

Joel Andrews
JA-VF, Joel Andrews, 245 East Mountain Ave., Santa Barbara, CA 93108

Violet Joy, Violet Flame

The violet flame of purification channeled through the harp of Joel Andrews. During the recording process, calling forth the flame is said to have produced a loud hum in the studio equipment and burned a hole in the cloud cover over the building.

DIE NACHT DER SEELE/ TANTRIC SONGS

Popol Vuh
Brain 0060.242 (A compilation of Tantric Songs and Brüder des Schattens, Söhne des Lichts is available as Celestial Harmonies 005)

edited version

Tantric Mayan German space music. Dark, serious, ritual/processional music for monks, piano, guitar and percussion.

The 'genesis' legends, or 'cosmogonies,' of Ethiopia tell of the origins of language, of how the first men could only sing — like the wind in the reeds — but how gradually they forgot the tune and had eventually to make do simply with the speaking of words.

Lawrence Blair

Music is a thing of the soul—a rose-lipped shell that murmured of the eternal sea—a strange bird singing the songs of another shore.

Josiah Gilbert Holland

BEHIND ELEVEN DESERTS

Stephan Micus
Wind 001

entire album

Yet another virtuoso Micus album of acoustical meditation music, this featuring the suling (Balinese bamboo flute), bodhran (Irish hand drum), sarangi, sitar, steel string and Spanish guitars, and 4 tin whistles.

CONCERT JOURNEY

Larkin
Wind Sung Sounds, 1259 El Camino Real, Suite 9, Menlo Park, CA 94025

Larkin with Ancient Leaves

The purity of Larkin's flute blends with Michael Stearns' numinous, electronic Ancient Leaves to create an entirely new piece.

AGUIRRE

Popol Vuh
Cosmic Couriers Pld. SQ-6040

Aguirre I

Music for a film by Werner Herzog. Processional and ritual flavor. A very uneven album. but this piece is very good.

AUM

Chaitanya Hari Deuter
Kuckuck Stereo 009

Surat Shabda, Abraxas, Susani

Early Deuter album. More rhythmic, not as meditative. Some very good pieces, some so-so.

ANCIENT ECHOES

Georgia Kelly, Steven Halpern
SRI-783-H

Cairo Practice, Crotona

Steve Halpern on flute, piano and vocals and Georgia Kelly on harp seek to evoke resonances of ancient Greece, Egypt and China.

JOEL ANDREWS: LIVE CONCERTS 1978

Joel Andrews
unpublished

Concert 11/26/78, Cofu Estates, Mill Valley, California

Joel Andrews tuning to the collective vibration of his audience and channeling energies from other dimensions to create an inspiring composition-moment.

THE MUSIC OF CHEOPS

Steve Douglas
CH 1, Cheops Records, 1420 N. Beachwood Dr., Hollywood, CA 90028

Reflections Along the Nile, Meditations at Luxor, Journey from Atlantis, Ascent

Solo saxophone improvisations in the King's chamber of the Great Pyramid. Ancient sounding with a jazz influence. Seems like a similar concept to Paul Horn's later album, although generally less meditative and more impressionistic.

After silence that which comes nearest to expressing the inexpressible is music.

Aldous Huxley

CELESTIAL VIBRATION

Edward Larry Gordon
SWN-52824

Bethlehem

First album of meditative zither music. Edward Larry Gordon is the Laraaji of Ambient #3: Day of Radiance.

OFFRANDES (OFFERINGS)

Cyrille Verdeaux
Soundings of the Planet, P. O. Box 43512, Tucson, AZ 85733

The Spell of the Sea; Remember Jonathan, the Seagull; Astral Trip

Considered as a whole, this is an interesting experience of echoes through many mystical traditions — planetary and interdimensional in scope — from this French musician. Primarily electronic with acoustic highlights.

RELATED MUSIC

ECLIPSE

Hamza El Din
Pacific Arts PACR7-119

OFFERINGS TO THE STARS: A ZITHER PERFORMANCE BY TSENG TA-YU

Tseng Ta-Yu
East-West Art Studio, 2530 Anza St., San Francisco, CA 94118

CELESTIAL ASCENT

Don Robertson
Don Robertson, 122 Steiner Court, Santa Rosa, CA 95404

THE OBLIQUE FLUTE

Richard Gerevich
HS 792, Halpern Sounds, 620 Taylor Way, #14, Belmont, CA 94002

SPACEFIELD

Malachi
Mu Tapes, P. O. Box 3966, Santa Rosa, CA 95402
Field Alpha, Field Beta, Field Delta, Field Gamma

TRANSCENDENTAL ROMANTIC

Expressive, emotion-creating music which opens one to higher experiences of beauty, peace, or communion.

SAMUEL BARBER: ADAGIO FOR STRINGS

Academy of St. Martin-in-the-Fields/Neville Marriner
Argo ZRG-845

Adagio for Strings

The Queen Mother of sad, elegiac adagios and a tremendous experience for opening the heart.

RACHMANINOFF: PIANO CONCERTO NO. 2

Jean Phillipe Collard/Orchestre de Capitole de Toulouse/Michel Plasson
Connoisseur Society cassette 4002 (also available on record)

Adagio sostenuto

Sensuous and emotional familiar classic. Collard's performance must be definitive.

RAVEL/ PIANO CONCERTO IN G MAJOR, FALLA/ NIGHTS IN THE GARDENS OF SPAIN

Phillippe Entremont, piano/The Philadelphia Orchestra/Eugene Ormandy
Columbia ML-6629

Ravel: Piano Concerto in G Major, Adagio

Gentle, lyrical movement . . . astral ballet music.

OPERA SAUVAGE

Vangelis
Polydor 2473 105

entire album

A listener: "This gave me a feeling of being a spark of consciousness without a point of view, feeling like a star on a night that's absolutely clear, and yet the feeling was one in which the boundaries dissolved — both the clarity and the dissolving boundaries at the same time." Yes. Really an excellent album.

IGNACIO (formerly CAN YOU HEAR THE DOGS BARKING?)

Vangelis Papathanassiou
Bellaphon BLPS-19242

(We play an edited tape of the Hearts parts — i.e., no cosmic bombast)

An early film soundtrack. Very lush synthesizer and keyboard sound. Recently used as the cosmic journey music for Carl Sagan's PBS series, Cosmos.

LA FETE SAUVAGE

Vangelis Papathanassiou
EMI C-066-14276

(edited version for Hearts of Space)

Very dreamy and romantic. Soundtrack for documentary film.

AARON COPLAND CONDUCTS HIS CLARINET CONCERTO, BENNY GOODMAN, SOLOIST

Copland conducting the Columbia Symphony Strings
Columbia MS 6497

Concerto for Clarinet and String Orchestra (with Harp and Piano), first movement

Tender, graceful space ballet.

BIG SUR TAPESTRY

Charles Lloyd, with Georgia Kelly, harp
Pacific Arts PAC 7-139

Partington Cove, Partington Point, Hill of the Hawk

High and airy, side 1 is one of the loveliest flute experiences available.

Music is the mediator between the spiritual and the sensual life.

Beethoven

THE PAVILION OF DREAMS

Harold Budd
Obscure OBS-10

Bismillah 'Rrahmani 'Rrahim, Madrigals of the Rose Angel

Very soft, relaxing and beautiful music from a California composer. Saxophone, space piano, wordless vocals. Produced by Brian Eno.

CLAIRE DE LUNE:
CLASSICS IN A ROMANTIC MOOD

Morton Gould
Quintessence PMC 7025

Beethoven: Moonlight Sonata (Adagio sostenuto)

The value of this hauntingly beautiful music overshadows its cliche status. This is a version transcribed for orchestra, using all its mellifluous romantic possibilities.

SEAPEACE

Georgia Kelly
Heru Records, P. O. Box 954, Topanga, CA 90290

Seapeace, Nilapadmam (Blue Lotus)

Georgia Kelly's first, excellent album of impressionistic harp meditations. Seapeace, with Tony Selvage's electric violin, is especially beautiful.

TARASHANTI

Georgia Kelly
Heru Records (see Seapace listing)

Marupavana, Tarashanti

Georgia's second album, also excellent. Marupavana has breaths of night-blooming magic . . . Moorish desert dreams. Tarashanti is elegantly Indian.

HEAVEN AND HELL

Vangelis Papathanassiou
RCA LPL1-5110

(The heavenly parts)

The best example of the extreme dynamic contrasts in Vangelis' music. The heavenly parts are essential Vangelis. Also used in the PBS Cosmos series.

L'APOCALYPSE DES ANIMAUX

Vangelis Papathanassiou
Polydor 2393-058

La Petite Fille de la Mer, Le Singe Bleu, La Mort du Loup, Creation de la Monde, La Mer Recommencee

Another film soundtrack. Shorter pieces, some very beautiful.

GO FOR BAROQUE

The Jean Francois Paillard Chamber Orchestra
RCA VICS-1687, or Musical Heritage Society MHS-1060

Pachelbel: Canon in D for Strings and Continuo

The richest, softest version of this gentle opening for the heart.

HOVHANESS: MYSTERIOUS MOUNTAIN

Chicago Symphony Orchestra/ Fritz Reiner
RCA LSC-22551

Andante, Andante con moto

One of the most popular symphonic works of this great contemporary American composer evokes the mystic grandeur of high places. There are probably better recordings available.

I am convinced that there are universal currents of Divine Thought vibrating the ether everywhere and that anyone who can feel these vibrations is inspired provided he is conscious of the process and possesses the knowledge and skill to present them . . . I have very definite impressions while in the trance-like condition which is the prerequisite of all true creative effort. I feel that I am one with this vibrating Force, that it is omniscient, and that I can draw upon it to an extent that is limited only by my own capacity to do so . . . One supreme fact which I have discovered is that it is not will-power but fantasy imagination that creates . . . Imagination is the creative force . . . imagination creates the reality.

Richard Wagner

BRUNO WALTER'S WAGNER

Bruno Walter and The Columbia Symphony Orchestra
Odyssey Y-30667

The Prelude to Lohengrin

Wagner's soaring, titanic vision of The Quest. Tremendously and tremulously romantic.

BIRDS OF PARADISE

Georgia Kelly, with Richard Hardy, flute
HERU 103, Heru Records, P. O. Box 954, Topanga, CA 90290

Birds of Paradise

Another in a series of excellent albums by Georgia Kelly, this a sensuous and lovely dance of feeling-tones for harp and flute.

CRYSTAL LOVE

Iasos
Iasos, P. O. Box 479, Waldo Pt., Sausalito, CA 94965

Oh, How Deeply Do I Love You?

A charming, tender episode featuring a virtuoso solo chirping performance by an ecstatically happy Marin County bird.

WILDERNESS AMERICA/ A CELEBRATION OF THE LAND

David Riordan, Peter Scott, Tom Salisbury
China Clipper Associates VEC 212

Water Cycle

A special grant-funded album of excellent quality. Semi-classical nature music alternating with eco-topical songs.

PARADISE SYMPHONY

Ralph Lundsten
Harvest 7C 062-35725

The Region of Heavenly Peace

This grand music is found within a collection of some of the corniest cosmic schlock ever devised. Ralphus Rex (as he calls himself) is talented, his sound quality is always first rate, but his concepts are pure Disneyland.

Oh, how beautiful it is to be alive — would that I could live a thousand times.

Beethoven

Contemporary electronic music in which the "space" is an integral part of the sound.

NADA

Peter Michael Hamel
Celestial Harmonies 001

Nada, Beyond the Wall of Sleep, Silence, Slow Motion

Refined use of synthesizer and virtuoso keyboard technique produce a powerful album of inner space music by a German composer who has gone deeply into the mysticism of sound, and whose book, Through Music to the Self, is a definitive work.

STARSCAPES

Geoffrey Chandler
Unity Records UR 706

Elysium Horizon, Iris, Stellar Solitude, Penumbra, The Celestial Divine

One of the finest painters of visionary spacescapes, Geoffrey Chandler is able to bring back both the images and sounds of the far reaches of deep space. His first album contains beautiful electronic portraits of star realms and eternal motions.

NEW AGE OF EARTH

Manuel Gottsching & Ash Ra Tempel
Isadora ISA-9003

Ocean of Tenderness, Nightdust

Mature Ash Ra at the transition from their hardcore space music to electronic pop. Lyrical and excellent throughout, these pieces are Hearts of Space standards.

ASH RA TEMPEL VI: INVENTIONS FOR ELECTRIC GUITAR

Manuel Gottsching
Cosmic Couriers KM 58.015

Quasarsphere, Pluralis

Spacey solo album with all sounds derived from electric guitar. Pluralis is an extended space journey. Quasarsphere is a lovely lullaby which served as our ending theme for years and was inexplicably dropped from the new pressings of this album.

TONTO'S EXPANDING HEAD BAND/ ZERO TIME

Robert Margouleff & Malcolm Cecil
Embryo SD-732

Tama, Riversong

Pioneer electronic pop album. Music ranges from threatening metal to gorgeous space lullabies. Excellent vocal processing on Riversong.

COMPUTER DON'T BREAK DOWN

Don Slepian
Don and Judy Records, 212 Summit Ave., Summit, N.J. 07901

Sonic Perfume, Judy's Rose

Don Slepian's first record (versus earlier cassettes) album shows the broad extent of his music from meditation to electronic bluegrass. Sonic Perfume is a scintillating, refreshing three-dimensional matrix of tonalities which seems to shower the listener with points of light. An unusual and promising album from an eclectic genius.

EVENING STAR

Fripp & Eno
Antilles AN-7018

Wind on Water, Evening Star, Evensong, Wind on Wind

A great mellow album of electric guitar, synthesizers and studio magic.

ANOTHER GREEN WORLD

Brian Eno
Island ILPS-9351

Becalmed, Zawinul/Lava, Spirits Drifting

Quixotic experimental album by Eno with some unsuccessful tracks and these three beauties.

AJATUSLAPSI

Esa Kotilainen
Love Records LRLP-196

Ilmassa

Delicate, high space composition from Finland.

BRUDER DES SCHATTENS, SOHNE DES LICHTS (BROTHER OF CLOUDS, SON OF LIGHTS)

Popul Vuh
Brain 0060.167 (A compilation of Brüder des Schattens, Sohne des Lichts and Tantric Songs is available as Celestial Harmonies 005)

Dramatic, processional, Eastern mysterious quality achieved with Western instrumentation — piano, electric guitar, drums — and vocals.

RITUAL OF THE STARMAKER

Robert Orban
unpublished

Ritual of the Starmaker

Flagship of our collection of unknown masterworks. A magnificent and powerful processional and canon for synthesizer and orchestral percussion. Orban is the Bay Area's answer to Walter Carlos.

CLUSTER & ENO

Moebieus, Roedelius, Eno
Best. — Nr. Sky 010 LC 4435

Wehrmut, Für Luise

This collaboration between the German group, Cluster, and producer Brian Eno achieves variable results, including these fine pieces. Wehrmut has an unusual way of altering your space.

PERELANDRA

Kevin Braheny
unpublished

An early 8-track synthesizer and vocal piece. The softest of floatings.

RUBYCON

Tangerine Dream
Virgin International VI 2025

Rubycon

One of their best albums, post-psychedelic but pre-commercial with all the elements of their music present but not overstated.

*Space. The continual becoming:
invisible fountain from which all rhythms
flow and to which they must pass.
Beyond time or Infinity.*

—Frank Lloyd Wright

*Architecture is an
art . . . when one
consciously or
unconsciously
creates aesthetic
emotion in the
atmosphere, and
when this
environment
produces well
being. . . . I think
the ideal space
must contain
elements of
magic, serenity,
sorcery and
mystery.*

Luis Barragan

AQUA

Edgar Froese
Virgin VR13-111

Aqua

Electronic psychedelic underwater.

MORTON FELDMAN: THE EARLY YEARS

Morton Feldman
Music of our Time: Odyssey 32-16-0302

Piece for Four Pianos

American "avant garde" composer, one of the few
whose work can be called meditative and whose
music generally transcends intellectualism.

CHRYSALIDE

Michel Moulinie
ZAL 6441

Le Philtre d'Echordus, Lente Course

Generally good album with these two standouts by
this young French electronic musician.

NEW SOUNDS IN ELECTRONIC MUSIC

Pauline Oliveras
Music of our Time: Odyssey 32-16-0160

I of IV

Early piece by pioneer American electronic
composer which we use as a galactic background
environment.

AFFENSTUNDE

Popol Vuh
IC 58159

Long ago album of extended consciousness journeys
via Moog synthesizer, guitar and hand drums.
Recently reissued by Klaus Schulze on his Innovative
Communications label.

KLAUS SCHULZE LIVE

Klaus Schulze
Brain 0080.048

Heart

Double live album, for fans only — the music is not as
good as his studio compositions. Apparently Klaus
knows this, and has announced that this record
marks the end of live performances (for the moment)
so he can create "the music of the future."

COSMIC BEAM EXPERIENCE

Francisco
CBE-001

entire album

Genuine California primitive spacemusic, a
distillation of spaces evolved during hundreds of live
performances by this virtuoso electronic
percussionist and songwriter.

COEUR DE VERRE

Popul Vuh
Egg 900-536

Engel der Gegenwart (Angel of the Present)

Soundtrack for Werner Herzog film. Good music,
Eastern influenced.

Space sings
Every atom's galaxy
Humming motion's grand illusion
Through the house of heaven's stars
Passing songs beyond Polaris
Shining brightly in the suns
Eclipsed by planet's revolutions
Cooled in phasing moonlight orbits
Flowing water's coursing bloods
Through the scent of earth's bouquet
Beyond the crystal forms of firey things
And atmospheres that dance in rings.

Jordan de la Sierra

SNOWFLAKES ARE DANCING

Tomita
RCA ARL-1-0488

The Engulfed Cathedral, Footprints in the Snow

Tomita's first album, synthesizer adaptations of music by Debussy. Probably his least gimmicky and most satisfying.

WHISPERED VISIONS

Emerald Web (Bob Stohl, Kat Epple)
Emerald Web, 58 Roble Rd., Berkeley, CA 94707

entire cassette

Soft, clear, spacey acoustic/electronic album which generally creates a warm, pleasant atmosphere. Some space journeys also.

COLD NOSE/NASO FREDDO (SOUNDTRACK)

Franco Falsini
Polydor 2449-012

Synthesizer/guitar solo album from Italian progressive musician. Dark, melodic, hypnotic . . .

DURCH DIE WUSTE/DESERT

Hans-Joachim Roedelius
Sky Records Sky 014

Durch die Wüste

Spacey, a little trippy, indulgent and occasionally strange.

SPACEBORNE (SOUNDTRACK)

Doug McKechnie
unpublished tape

Soundtrack for an art film created from NASA footage of actual astronauts in real live Space. Effective and enjoyable music, mostly synthesizer.

RELATED MUSIC

CLOCKWORK ORANGE

Walter Carlos
Columbia KC 31480
Theme Music from A Clockwork Orange

INNER TRAVELOGUE

Joseph Adams
Joseph Adams, 10020 S. E. Mt. Scott, Portland, OR 97266
The Head Takes a Walk, Hang Gliding in the Canyons of Your Mind

Evolving, non-traditional music which sonically evokes the imagery of Infinite or Unlimited spacetime.

X

Klaus Schulze
Brain 0080.023

George Trakl, Ludwig II, Friedemann Bach, Heinrich Von Kleist

A masterpiece which is not only the quintessence of ten years of electronic music development, but firmly establishes Klaus as a serious composer intent on creating a new ''music of the future.''

SILK ROAD II (ORIGINAL SOUNDTRACK)

Kitaro
Canyon C25R0052 (Camel caravan cover)

entire album

Young master musician orchestrates numerous electronic instruments and traditional Japanese sounds into a rich cosmic tapestry. A thoroughly mature, satisfying presentation. His best.

SILK ROAD I (ORIGINAL SOUNDTRACK)

Kitaro
Canyon C25R0038 (Japanese gong cover)

entire album except Side A, #1

More energetic, not quite as smooth, but a very good album. Try to ignore the bizarre edit at the 2/3 mark of side one.

RAINBOW DOME MUSIK

Steve Hillage, Miquette Giraudy
Virgin VR-1

Garden of Paradise, Four Ever Rainbow

Good ''naturalized'' space music with guitar, synthesizer, Tibetan bells and ambient nature sounds. Everyone likes this album.

MIRAGE

Klaus Schulze
Island ILPS-9461

Crystal Lake

1978 Klaus Schulze winter crystal music. A kinetic deep space journey. One of his finest albums.

PICTURE MUSIC

Klaus Schulze
Brain 1067

Totem

Excellent electronic trance music. Spacey and delicately percussive, with an Indian music influence — Raga Cosmos.

MOONDAWN

Klaus Schulze
Brain 1088

Floating, Moondawn

Excellent middle period solo album with Klaus moving a step toward rock by reincorporating drums into his electronic toneworlds.

TIMEWIND

Klaus Schulze
Brain 1075

Bayreuth Return, Wahnfried 1883

Dedicated to Richard Wagner. Wahnfried good for stormy winter nights. Bayreuth is an extended, exciting space cruise.

DUNE

Klaus Schulze
Brain 0060.225

Shadows of Ignorance

A transitional album with Klaus Schulze searching for new directions after the masterful X double album of '78-'79. Features Arthur Brown's vocal/recitations of Klaus' futurist poetry. Extraordinary cello playing by Wolfgang Tiepold and brilliant sound.

HARMONIC ASCENDANT

Robert Schroeder
Innovative Communication IC 58 087U

Harmonic Ascendant

Excellent piece of hybrid electronic/acoustic space music produced by Klaus Schulze that orbits through several fields solidly supported by fine classical guitar and the cello work of Wolfgang Tiepold.

OASIS

Kitaro
Canyon C25R0030

Rising Sun, Moro-ism, New Wave, Cosmic Energy, Moon Light, Shimmering Horizon, Fragrance of the Nature, Innocent People

Skilled and graceful, Kitaro glides through several electronic styles. Great night-travelling music.

TIME ACTOR

Richard Wahnfried
Innovative Communication IC 58065

Time Actor, Time Factory, Charming the Wind, Grandma's Clockwork, Time Echoes

A "group" album produced and masterminded by Klaus Schulze. A successful attempt to create a new format for philosophical discourse (on the meaning of time) in an electronic setting. Last song contains a performance by a quasi-alien vocalist.

HERGEST RIDGE

Mike Oldfield
Virgin VR-13-109

entire album

This record has been mostly ignored, but it achieves a completely successful integration of rock, space, and English folk and pastoral musics. Really one of his best.

OMMADAWN

Mike Oldfield
Virgin PZ-33913 (out-of-print)

entire album

Another excellent electronic/acoustic orchestration based on Celtic, English folk and rock influences by this young English composer/multi-instrumentalist.

OXYGENE

Jean Michel Jarre
Polydor 2933-207

Part I, Part II, Part III, Part V

The first electronic "space music" album to hit big commercially, it created a standard to which popular space albums will be compared. Music ranges from deep romantic to space disco with full cinematic effects. Excellent production and sound.

EQUINOXE

Jean Michel Jarre
Polydor PD-16175

Parts 1, 2, 3, 4, 7

Jarre's second album of space flight music. A bizarre mixture of styles that creates an enjoyable result.

FROM THE FULL MOON STORY

Kitaro
Zen-1006

entire album, except Bali

An album that would be a masterpiece by anyone else and is grade B by this artist's standards. Basically the same sound/music arrangement as the others but more acoustic.

TEN KAI (ASTRAL TRIP)

Kitaro
Zen 1001 (Japan Victor)

Entire album except Mu

High quality Japanese acoustic/electronic mix by a Klaus Schulze protege.

TUBULAR BELLS

Mike Oldfield
Virgin 13-105

entire album

The one which made him famous when adapted for the soundtrack of The Exorcist. A fresh sound for its time, with a dash of droll English humor injected by narrator Vivian Stanshall.

INCANTATIONS

Mike Oldfield
Virgin 300-193-420

entire 2 discs, especially side 4

Oldfield's fourth album, produced and largely performed by him, synthesizing widely varied musical traditions and instrumentation into a truly original work — this one from African drums to the Queens College Girls Choir.

STRATOSFEAR

Tangerine Dream
Virgin V2068

3 a.m. at the Border of the Marsh from Okefenokee, Invisible Limits, The Big Sleep in Search of Hades

Mature album. Excellent production and sound. 3 a.m. fits into an informal Hearts category called "weird harmonic."

IN THE REGIONS OF SUNRETURN

Michael Garrison
Windspell Records WS 112856

Dreams, The Distance from Here

First album by a talented young synthesist from Oregon. Derivative of the major European artists but very enjoyable music.

RAINBOW DELTA

Patrick Gleeson
PVC 7914

5:10 to Dreamland

The most meditative piece on this up-to-date sounding synthesizer album by a San Francisco producer/composer.

Music is another planet.

Alphonse Daudet

Space! That response to the aspiration of the human being, that relaxation for breathing and for the beating heart, that outpouring of self in looking far, from a great height, over a vast, infinite, unlimited expanse.
— Le Corbusier

PLATINUM

Mike Oldfield
Virgin V2141

Woodhenge, North Star

Some nice music from a more experimental album which covers many different styles including disco.

KOSMOS

Tomita
RCA ARL-1-2616

The Sea Named Solaris

Tomita's space concept album. Fanciful, occasionally excessive but interesting free adaptations of music by Bach, Strauss, Wagner, Honegger, Ives, Grieg and Rodrigo.

BOLERO

Tomita
RCA ARL1-3412

A good album of electronic transcriptions of music by Ravel.

HELDON 2

Heldon/Richard Pinhas
Disjuncta 000002

St. Mikael Samstag Abends, In the Wake of King Fripp

A guitar/synthesizer album from a French radical artist and political philosopher whose music ranges from irritating to a kind of harsh, spacey beauty.

RELATED MUSIC

ALBEDO 0.39

Vangelis
RCA RS-1080
Albedo 0.39

PHAEDRA

Tangerine Dream
Virgin VR 13-108

CYCLONE

Tangerine Dream
Virgin V2097

DEPARTURE FROM THE NORTHERN WASTELAND

Michael Hoenig
Warner Bros. BSK 3152

BENZAITEN

Osamu Kitajima
Antilles AN-7016
Triyo — The Sun

OSA-MU

Osamu Kitajima
Island ILPS-9426

MACULA TRANSFER

Edgar Froese
Brain 60.008
os 452, quantas 611

IRRLICHT

Klaus Schulze
Brain 1077
Ebene, Gewitter

TANGRAM

Tangerine Dream
Virgin V2147
Side 2, Tangram set 2 (edited)

Repetition is the image of eternity in music.
Michael Hoenig

PICTURE MUSIC

Klaus Schulze
Brain LP-1067

Totem

Spacey piece of cyclic trance music featuring a unique "electronic tabla" sound, a rhythmic yet gentle intramolecular massage. As close as Klaus ever came to Indian music.

SHRI CAMEL

Terry Riley
CBS Masterworks M35164

Anthem of the Trinity, Celestial Valley, Across the Lake of the Ancient Word, Desert of Ice

Terry Riley's most recent (1980) album of virtuoso organ/synthesizer improvisations. Somewhat more tonal variety, but still ancient and austere sounding.

MUSIC OF XOLOTL

Xolotl
Unity Records UR 702

Morning Glory, Phase Aurora, Comet Falling
Journey to an Oracle, Magenta Deep Anemones
(unpublished tapes)

Cyclic music with more sensual textures via electric guitar and recycled delays from a French composer and gifted visual artist. Organ accompaniment on some pieces.

HOLOGRAMS

Margaret Fabrizio
unpublished tape

Impeccably focused musical figures varied and repeated on the harpsichord to produce deep inner states. Margaret Fabrizio's work should be recorded and made available.

PERSIAN SURGERY DERVISHES

Terry Riley
Shandar 83.501/502

entire album

A fine two-record set of live electronic organ/tape delay meditations by a Western musician. This music was used as the soundtrack for a French documentary on the whirling dervishes.

JOURNEY FROM THE DEATH OF A FRIEND

Terry Riley
Warner Bros.

Journey from the Death of a Friend

Another Terry Riley film soundtrack similar to the others. This piece seems special, though. Electronic organ.

RAINBOW IN CURVED AIR/POPPY NOGOOD AND THE PHANTOM BAND

Terry Riley
Columbia MS-7315

entire album

Probably his most popular album, dating from the late '60s. A mature statement of his music with a rich ensemble texture. The one to get if you're getting 1.

GYMNOSPHERE: SONG OF THE ROSE

Jordan de la Sierra
Unity Records (double album version) UR 701

Tihai: In the Realm of Rama IX

Thirty minutes of a 33 note cyclic pattern played on the spatially expanded piano. Takes you ever so deep.

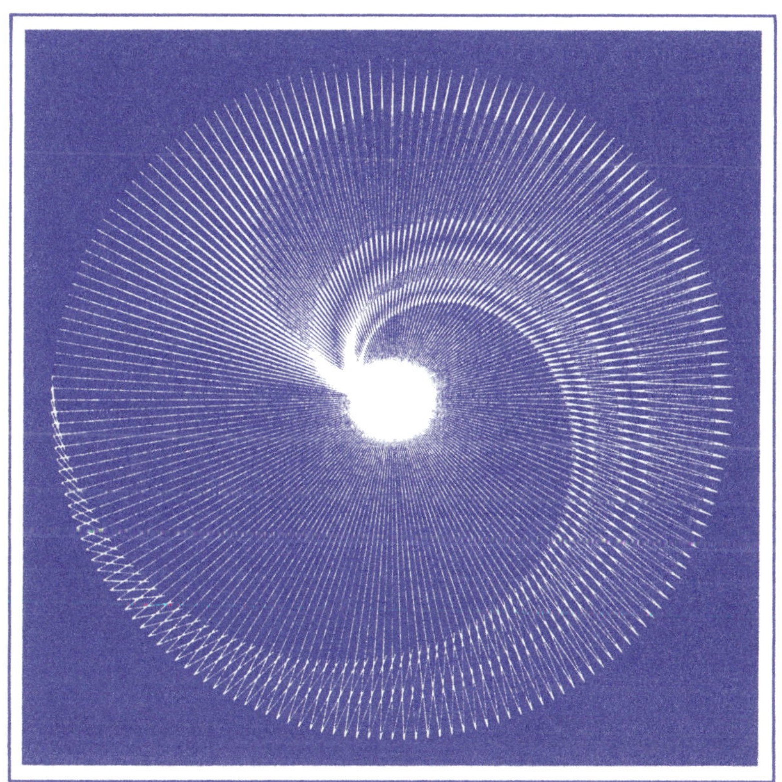

NORTH STAR

Phillip Glass
Virgin PZ-34669

North Star

Interesting music from a New York composer who has won enthusiastic audiences for his cyclic ensemble music in many live performances. Sound ranges from irritating to transcendent and is always hypnotic. Electric keyboards, vibraphone, glockenspiel, saxophones, voices.

LIFESPAN (LA SECRET DE LA VIE)

Terry Riley
STIP ST 1011 (Disques Sonopresse, dist.)

In the Summer

Yet another film soundtrack, a collection of shorter pieces, some very rich. Multi-voice electronic organ sound.

DOUBLE HELIX; PATTERNS

Doug McKechnie
unpublished tapes

Short cyclic pieces for synthesizer by San Francisco composer/multi media artist Doug McKechnie.

RELATED MUSIC

MUSIC FOR 18 MUSICIANS

Steve Reich
Warner Bros. ECM-1-1129

OCTET, MUSIC FOR A LARGE ENSEMBLE, VIOLIN PHASE

Steve Reich
ECM-1-1168

Music and rhythm find their way into the secret places of the soul

Plato

CELLULAR WAVE MUSIC

A category created for the subtle movement meditation music of the Continuum Studio, used for deep journeys into the body.

At the heart of each of us, whatever our imperfections, there exists a silent pulse of perfect rhythm, a complex of wave forms and resonances, which is absolutely individual and unique, and yet which connects us to everything in the universe. The act of getting in touch with this pulse can transform our personal experience and in some way alter the world around us.

George Leonard, ***The Silent Pulse***

MORNING/JEWEL

Michael Stearns
Continuum Montage, 3640-1/2 Watseka Ave., Los Angeles, CA 90034 (cassette only)

Jewel, Morning

Jewel, a blend of wordless voices and shimmering warm tones created on the Eikosany vibes, is an extraordinarily high piece of music. Morning combines nature sounds recorded at dawn in an Arizona desert and Mexican jungle with acoustical, vocal and electronic music. It's especially good on Sunday morning.

LULLABY FOR THE HEARTS OF SPACE/AFTER I SAID GOODNIGHT

Kevin Braheny
Heartcall Music, P.O. Box 3565, Santa Monica, CA 90403

Lullaby for the Hearts of Space, After I Said Goodnight

Exquisite journeys for synthesizer and soprano sax. The music flows from the inside out. Lullaby was created live, on-the-air, during a special Hearts of Space program.

ANCIENT LEAVES

Michael Stearns
Continuum Montage, 3640-1/2 Watseka Ave., Los Angeles, CA 90034

Ancient Leaves, Elysian E

Michael Stearns' first album integrates electronic drones, chanting, modal string music. Continuum well describes Elysian E as "a moving chordal sea," and Ancient Leaves as "a journey through inner space where sound worlds emerge, unfold and dissolve."

PICNIC AT HANGING ROCK

Michael Stearns
Continuum Montage (unpublished)

Picnic at Hanging Rock

A montage of synthesizer ambience and the extraordinary pan pipes of Gheorghe Zamfir create a very special moment.

*Motion is the
nature of
vibration. Every
motion contains
within itself a
thought and a
feeling.*

Hazrat Inayat Khan

THE SOFT TOUCH OF MORNING LIGHT
MARRIAGE CHORDS

Michael Stearns
Continuum Montage (to be published)

Soft Touch: This synthesizer music is mysteriously effective — quiet yet active — soothing yet stimulating. It creates an ambience which can be sustained for hours. Marriage Chords: A rich ascent, written by Michael Stearns for his own marriage.

SUSTAINING CYLINDERS,
SLEEPING CONCHES

Michael Stearns
Continuum Montage (cassette only)

Sustaining Cylinders, Sleeping Conches

Two specialized electronic meditation sound environments. Sustaining Cylinders was created on the Eikosany vibes (22 tones to the octave). In Sleeping Conches sounds of the ocean are combined with bells and conch shells. Unique healing sounds for quiet work.

A M B I E N T

An ambience is defined as an atmosphere, or a surrounding influence: a tint. Whereas the extant canned music companies proceed from the basis of regularizing environments by blanketing their acoustic and atmospheric idiosyncracies, Ambient Music is intended to enhance these. Whereas conventional background music is produced by stripping away all sense of doubt and uncertainty (and thus all genuine interest) from the music, Ambient Music retains these qualities. And whereas their intention is to 'brighten' the environment by adding stimulus to it (thus supposedly alleviating the tedium of routine tasks and levelling out the natural ups and downs of the body rhythms) Ambient Music is intended to induce calm and a space to think. Ambient Music must be able to accommodate many levels of listening attention without enforcing one in particular; it must be as ignorable as it is interesting.

Brian Eno

AMBIENT #1: MUSIC FOR AIRPORTS

Brian Eno
PVC-7908
1/1, 2/1, 1/2
Excellent album of music to provide acoustic atmospheres for architectural spaces . . . which also open to inner spaces that have no enclosure.

AMBIENT #2: THE PLATEAUX OF MIRROR

Harold Budd/Brian Eno
E.G. Records, Ltd., EGS 202
entire album
Gentle, refined album of processed piano and synthesizer music. Just totally beautiful.

AMBIENT #3: DAY OF RADIANCE

Laraaji
Editions EG, EGAMB 003
Meditation #1, #2,
If this is an "atmosphere," it is a very, very deep one. An ambience like mahogany nights around ancient Asian fires, created with an electronically processed zither.

TUNED WIND/THE DRAGON WAITS

Kevin Braheny
not yet available
Tuned Wind, The Dragon Waits
Very deep synthesized inner space meditation/ambiences by an extremely sensitive composer.

MORTON FELDMAN

Morton Feldman
Odyssey Y-34138
Rothko Chapel
Tribute to painter Mark Rothko created for Houston's Rothko Chapel. Very spatial; with chorus, viola and percussion.

RELATED MUSIC

SPACE FOR STEPHEN

Alden Jenks
unpublished
Namo
Drones and electronic spaces for inner ambience.

SOUND SPACE ENVIRONMENTS

Natural and electronic sound environments which are not formally "music."

ENVIRONMENTS 3

Syntonic Research
LPSD-66003

Dusk at New Hope, Pennsylvania

The Hearts of Space cricket choir.

ENVIRONMENTS 7

Syntonic Research
SD-66007

Intonation

A half-hour of layered, cascading OM sound. It takes one deeply into harmony.

SONIC SEASONINGS

Walter Carlos
Columbia KG-31234

entire album, especially Winter

Superb "aural tapestry" of natural and electronic sounds to evoke the four seasons. A pioneer work.

ENVIRONMENTS 1

Syntonic Research
LPSD-66001

The Ultimate Seashore

Synthesized ocean, but a very effective idealization of the real thing.

SONOMA SURF, SOFT

Lou Judson
Intuitive Audio, P. O. Box 655, Larkspur, CA 94939

One of the most beautiful recordings of gentle night sea.

THE WIND HARP: SONG FROM THE HILL

The Wind Harp
United Artists UAS-9963

entire album

Indescribable sounds created by a wind harp erected in the northeastern U.S.
"Sometimes
she sounds like a ghostly house
and sometimes
like a flying saucer
but mostly
she sounds like everything singing
far, far away."

ENVIRONMENTS 10

Syntonic Research
SD-66010

Night in the Country

Soothing ambience, yet made up of 1000 discrete insect sounds in complex patterings.

THE LANGUAGE AND MUSIC OF WOLVES ·

Tonsil Records

Bands 5, 10

Magnificent calls, bringing deep stirrings of connection. Sing with your wolf brother.

SONGS OF THE HUMPBACK WHALE

Capitol ST-620

entire album

Classic record by Dr. Roger Payne of the ethereal calls of great beings.

What makes us feel drawn to music is that our whole being is music; our mind and body, the nature in which we live, the nature which has made us, all that is beneath and around us, it is all music; and we are close to all this music, and live and move and have our being in music.

Hazrat Inayat Khan

Listen to the sound of the river. In it are contained all voices, the sum of all sound, all the cries and laughter of the world.

Herman Hesse, **Siddartha**

I love music passionately. . . . It is a free art gushing forth, an open-air art boundless as the elements, the wind, the sky, the sea. . . . Music is the expression of the movement of the waters, the play of curves described by changing breezes. There is nothing more musical than a sunset. He who feels what he sees will find no more beautiful example of development than in the book of Nature.

Claude Debussy

DEEP VOICES: THE SECOND WHALE RECORD

Capitol ST-11598

Left Over Sea Running, Drifting Off, Deep Voices, Deep Breathing

More whale songs, lovely and mysterious, recorded underwater by Roger and Katy Payne. Proceeds from this and the first whale record go to help save the whales.

ENVIRONMENTS 4

Syntonic Research
LPSD-66004

Gentle Rain in a Pine Forest

Summer rain with occasional birdsongs.

ENVIRONMENTS 2

Syntonic Research
Atlantic SD-66002

Tintinnabulation, Dawn at New Hope

Soft bells and the morning joy of birds.

VIBRATIONAL ENVIRONMENTS #4: THRONE REALMS AND LAGOONS

Iasos
Iasos, P. O. Box 479, Waldo Pt., Sausalito, CA 94965

Throne Realms

Vast space, vast power in a state of calm rest.

ENVIRONMENTS 5

Syntonic Research
SD-66005

Wind in the Trees

Pastoral sound imagery of a gentle autumn day.

ENVIRONMENTS 8

Syntonic Research
LPSD-66008

Country Stream

Very alive water sounds.

RELATED MUSIC

TANK TAPE

Ed Doyle and Rich Candib
unpublished tape

Tank #1

Flute and voice cosmically reverberating inside a water tank off Highway 80 near Sacramento.

VIBRATIONAL ENVIRONMENTS #3: BIRDS FOR MORNING AND EVENING

Iasos
Iasos, P. O. Box 479, Waldo Pt., Sausalito CA 94965

VIBRATIONAL ENVIRONMENTS #5: ESSENCE OF SPRING

Iasos
Iasos, P. O. Box 479, Waldo Pt., Sausalito, CA 94965

The Descent of Spring

According to Iasos, this piece carries with it the vibration of Amaryllis, the Goddess of Spring, and her orchestration of the energies of that season.

HEAVEN ON EARTH

Schawkie Roth
Center of Heavenly Music, P. O. Box 1063, Larkspur, CA 94939

Heaven on Earth

Joyful, fluid meditative piece for zither, flute, saxophone, voice and natural sounds.

NORDIC NATURE SYMPHONY #2: JOHANNES AND THE LADY OF THE WOODS

Ralph Lundsten
Odeon (EMI) E 061-35200

The Enchanted Forest, The Lady of the Woods Calls in the Summer Night, And Autumn Came

One of Lundsten's most restrained and beautiful albums. Evokes the spirit of the earth in a familiar European fairytale style.

RELATED MUSIC

DESERT DAWN SONG

Soundings of the Planet
Earthlab/Soundings of the Planet, 405 N. Wilson, Tucson, AZ 85719

OF THE DOVE AND OF THE ROSE

Sananda
Earthlab/Soundings of the Planet, 405 N. Wilson, Tucson, AZ 85719

Some people say it's a dichotomy that I'm trying to create organic nature music and yet I'm using all these electronics. What could be more organic than electrons? What do you think a flower's made of? I think of electrons as these very, very tiny God-beings that are extremely sensitive to consciousness and are just rushing — literally at the speed of light — just to fulfill your will. All these wires are just creating different paths. You tell the electrons which way you want them to go, and they jump at the chance to serve. They go exactly where you want them to. So I think of them as my joyous little servants. They just love to do whatever I want . . .

Iasos

ETHERIC TROPICAL

Music which evokes the enveloping essence of our earthly paradise gardens.

VIBRATIONAL ENVIRONMENTS #2: EARTH CALM/SPACE CALM

Iasos
Iasos, P. O. Box 479, Waldo Pt., Sausalito, CA 94965

Kona Jungle, Cloud Prayer

Iasos describes Kona Jungle as having ''a deep, archetypal, mysterious feeling—low musical tones surrounded by a very rich texture of nature sounds which tend to induce alpha in the listener.'' It has the power of the heart of the night.

OSMOSE

Ariel Kalma & Richard Tinti
Societe Francaise de Productions Phonographiques-Paris SFP 3.5021-5022

entire album, except Saxo Planetariel, 6 and C, Manege, Gongmo

The ultimate etheric tropical environment. Jungle environment tapes recorded in Borneo, then mixed with electronic sound. Beautifully pressed 2-record set.

BALI AGUNG

Eberhard Schoener
Celestial Harmonies 002

Tjandra, Nadi, Ramayana, Surya

German synthesizer musician meets Balinese gamelan orchestra. Deep earth magic.

INTER-DIMENSIONAL MUSIC THROUGH IASOS

Iasos
Iasos, P. O. Box 479, Waldo Pt., Sausalito, CA 94965

Creation/Cloud Prayer, Crystal Petals, Sirens Shallows, Formantera Sunset Clouds, Lagoon Night

From the Temple of Crystal Fire Radiance, Iasos synthesizes music played to him from other dimensions. In this, his first album, he explores a variety of inter-dimensional environments.

Here you hear every sound you make, and, to the depth of your stillness, every sound you are . . . The Hawaiian wind is a great Being. It unifies the night, soaring majestically off the pali, sending off long crescendos which then burst forth multitudes of song tendrils. They are indeed, in the most literal sense, wind sung sounds. And since everything here is multi-sensorial, the wind's songs are heard, experienced, on the skin delicately, with exquisite softness. The wind brings healing, encircling you so rapidly you feel all of your skin at once, touching with slender strokes. . . . lightening and soothing.

*You are surrounded by subtle cascades of shifting fragrance — enchanting, purifying scents that **are** music. You flow through nights of a thousand flowers: trees everywhere full of intoxicating plumeria; languid, brazen hibiscus; delicate, etheric white spidery lilies; shimmering white ginger; and tiny lavender buds, coiled so powerfully, in such perfect alignment with some universal spirals of energy, that it feels as if each flowering could produce ripples galaxies away.*

*We **are** starflower beings. It is profound to be so close. . . .*

Annamystyq
Hawaii, 1978

IN DEN GÄRTEN PHARAOS

Popul Vuh
Cosmic Couriers pld. SQ-6009

In den Gärten Pharaos

An evocation of ancient steamy jungle garden nights. Rousseau might have painted it.

EPSILON IN MALAYSIAN PALE

Edgar Froese
Virgin V-2040

Epsilon in Malaysian Pale

Not strictly etheric tropical, this is more of an interpretation of that feeling in the tradition of Western reflections upon natural settings — this one using electronic textures, flute and environmental effects.

THE ROMANCE OF HAWAII

Webeley Edwards and Hal Arnell
Pickwick: Hawaii Calls series (out of print)

Fire Goddess

True magic in a chant to the Fire Goddess, Pele. If anyone has a good copy of this, please write.

FETE DES BELLES EAUX

Jeanne Loriod & Ensemble
Musical Heritage Society 821-L

excerpt

Composed by Olivier Messiaen and performed by an ensemble of Ondes Martenots, early vacuum-tube synthesizers of exquisitely refined tonality. Almost unbearably beautiful.

JEWEL / MORNING

Michael Stearns
Continuum Montage, 3640-1/2 Watseka Ave., Los Angeles, CA 90034

Jewel

A deceptively simple synthesizer tone leads you to the gentlest of transcendent realms. A deeply powerful work.

HALEAKALA

Chaitanya Hari Deuter
Kuckuck 2375-042

Haleakala Mystery

A piece inspired by the summits of Hawaii's ancient volcano, Haleakala. Voices, synthesizers and high awareness. A rarefied experience . . . unsurpassed.

AMBIENT #3: DAY OF RADIANCE

Laraaji
Editions EG, EGAMB 003

Meditation #1, #2

One of our most mystical pieces. Deeply and profoundly relaxing music for electronically treated zither by this musician/priest. Produced by Brian Eno. We thank you.

SONG OF THE GOLDEN LOTUS

Swami Kriya Ramananda
Satsanga Fellowship, Box 6165, Chicago, IL 60680

Devata

An intensely beautiful meditation for the heart. Composed and performed on bass flute and synthesizer (with some cello accompaniment) by a young American Self Realization Fellowship monk.

TIBETAN BELLS II

Henry Wolff and Nancy Hennings
Celestial Harmonies 006

White Light, Astral Plane

These are intense, high frequency meditations, highlights of an album of original music played on Tibetan instruments. "If you listen long and hard down into the bells you will either go insane or be propelled towards enlightenment." — Tibetan lama.

GYMNOSPHERE: SONG OF THE ROSE

Jordan de la Sierra
Unity UR-701

Side 3 of double album version

Ancient Babylonian spacemusic — a dark, rich, harmonic sound from a specially tuned, electronically processed piano. Deep . . .

MUSIC OF OUR TIME: EXTENDED VOICES

Morton Feldman
Odyssey 32-16-0156

Chorus and Instruments (II), Christian Wolff in Cambridge

Music for space chorus, tuba and chimes whose slow, extended breaths create a perfect meditative ambience. May be heard as set in the far spacefields with intimations of the grand wheelings of stars, or on an innerspace plane.

HEARTCALL

Kevin Braheny
presently unpublished

Heartcall

Yearning, evocative heartcallings — perfectly named — on the Mighty Serge Synthesizer and soprano sax.

SONG OF THE PEAKS

Maggi Payne
Center for Contemporary Music, P. O. Box 9991, Mills College, Oakland, CA 94613

Song of the Peaks

Soaringly beautiful ascents, glides and hoverings for flute and gong and electronics. Composed by William Maraldo, performed by Maggi Payne.

MUSIC BY JOANNA BROUK

Joanna Brouk
Hummingbird Productions, P. O. Box 9871, Oakland, CA 94613

Gong Piece, Conch

Deep synthesizer evocations of the essence of a conch shell and the universal resonances of the gong.

CRYSTAL LOVE

Iasos
Iasos, P. O. Box 479, Waldo Pt., Sausalito, CA 94965

Crystal*White*Fire*Light

Dazzling sweeps of shimmering sound designed by Iasos and the Beings for whom he serves as an earth transmission point ''to accelerate one's forcefield into crystalline octaves of consciousness and to accelerate one's emotional body into crystalline octaves of joy.'' Advanced.

M A N T R A Traditional, (mostly) Eastern, cyclic religious chanting.

Concentration frees the mind for union.

Old Hindu Sutra

CHO-GA: TANTRIC AND RITUAL MUSIC OF TIBET

Tibetan Monks from Northern India & Nepal
Dorje-Ling Records, Box 1410, San Rafael, CA 94902

Chi-lu

The sounds of the mountain moving. Real, authentic, terrific recordings, a variety of music.

TIBETAN RITUAL MUSIC

Lamas and Monks of Tibet
Lyrichord LLST-7181

Invocation of Gompo

Deep choruses of Tibetan monks.

AHI

Bhagavan Das
Pacific Arts PACR 7-111

Ah!

Bhagavan Das, son of Laguna Beach, Eastern seeker, ancient soul, sings with his heart to the Cosmic Mother. A one disc reissue of the original two-record set.

THE RADHA KRSHNA TEMPLE

The Radha Krshna Temple, London
Apple SKAO-4476

Mantra meets folk rock. Produced by George Harrison.

(Hans Jenny, in the research he called Cymatics, the study of the interrelationship of wave-forms with matter) . . . built a 'tonoscope' which transforms sounds uttered into a microphone into their visual representation on a screen. The sacred Hindu syllable **Om,** *when correctly uttered into the tonoscope, apparently produces the circle* **O,** *which is then filled in with concentric squares and triangles, finally producing, when the last traces of the* **m** *have died away, a* **yantra** *– the formal geometrical expression of sacred vibration which is found in many of the world's religions . . . Here . . . is . . . evidence to suggest that the script – where it remains – of sacred, liturgical languages (such as High Javanese or Hebrew) bears a much closer resemblance to its forms in the tonoscope than do the commonly spoken languages of today. If confirmed, this supports the theory that liturgical language and music supplied not only a special vocabulary through which the ancient priest classes could speak of different realities, but a vocabulary which itself resonated to the vibrations it described.*

Lawrence Blair, **Rhythms of Vision**

THE HEALING JOURNEY

Rafiel
Emmett Miller, M.D., 945 Evelyn, Menlo Park, CA 94025

Breathing Music

An unusually beautiful healing journey of the heart. Piano, chorus, flutes, zither, violins and tamboura. Extraordinarily moving, deeply releasing, with some powerful moments of emotional transcendence.

THE SEA OF BLISS

Don Slepian
Plumeria, I. M. Music Distributors, P. O. Box 54, Kailua, HI 96734

The Sea of Bliss, The Ocean of Peace

First album of meditative electronic music from an artist we feel has tremendous skill and potential. His music is already at the level of sonic and musical integration which few achieve — simultaneously stimulating and effervescent and soothing and profound. Programmed/performed on an advanced digital synthesizer.

VIBRATIONAL ENVIRONMENTS #1: ANGELIC MUSIC

Iasos
Iasos, P. O. Box 479, Waldo Pt., Sausalito, CA 94965

The Angels of Comfort, Angel Play

The Angels of Comfort is truly that — soothing, peaceful immersion into galactic love. Angel Play is correctly described as having ''an ethereally-playful feeling that tends to act as an emotional 'tenderizer' — softening and delicatizing any hardened emotions into greater pliability and sensitivity.''

MUSIC FOR ZEN MEDITATION

Tony Scott
Verve V6-8634

entire album

A classic album of music for clarinet, shakuhachi and koto to clear your mind and your space.

SONG OF THE GOLDEN LOTUS

Swami Kriya Ramananda
Satsanga Fellowship, Box 6165, Chicago, Illinois 60680

Devata, Song of the Golden Lotus, Wu Wei

One of the deepest and most beautiful albums of meditation music we have encountered. (See review under Mystical Vibratory Experiences.)

BHAGWAN SHREE RAJNEESH

BSR-1
Through Rajneesh centers. May be out of print.

Dervish Dancing (Sufi Whirling Meditation)

Harmonium/vocal/electronic music designed for Sufi whirling meditation, can be used for any form of meditation which is at once centered and expanding. This album was put together in California, we are told, from music supplied by Chaitanya Hari Deuter.

SONIC PERFUME #2

Don Slepian
Plumeria, I. M. Music Distributors, P. O. Box 54, Kailua, HI 96734

Awakening, Open Spaces

Don Slepian's second album. Similar music to Sea of Bliss in its cascading, layered toneworlds and its depth and beauty.

MUSIC OF THE SPHERES

Liv Singh Khalsa and Sat Want Kaur Khalsa
Guru Ram Das Recordings, P. O. Box 13054, Phoenix, AZ 85002

entire cassette

Side one features bells, tamboura, spacey flute, recorder, guitar and harmonium. Side two extends the meditation with a subtly changing drone that sounds electronic, but isn't. Both pieces are in Rag Bhairo and create a gentle, serene ambience. Good for meditation or just psycho-deceleration.

Sama . . . means literally 'hearing.' It is music used for travel purposes. Not for the mind to wander or fantasize, but with concentration to soar — out of this world into the unseen, and from there to the limits of the spatial . . . It is the heart's journey to the heart of the heart.

The Habibiyya

What is wonderful about music is that it helps man to concentrate or meditate independently of thought; and therefore music seems to be the bridge over the gulf between form and the formless. If there is anything intelligent, effective and at the same time formless, it is music. Poetry suggests form, line and colour suggest form, but music suggests no form. It creates also that resonance which vibrates through the whole being, lifting the thought above the denseness of matter; it almost turns matter into spirit, into its original condition, through the harmony of vibrations touching every atom of one's being.

Beauty of line and colour can go so far and no further; the joy of fragrance can go a little further; but music touches our innermost being and in that way produces new life, a life that gives exaltation to the whole being, raising it to that perfection in which lies the fulfillment of man's life.

Hazrat Inayat Khan

SOUND OF THE GONG

S. S. Nanak Dev Singh Khalsa
Guru Ram Das Recordings, P.O. Box 13054, Phoenix, AZ 85002

entire cassette, especially Side 2

A long and very powerful meditation with the ancient sound used in mystical traditions to experience the realms of the unknown. Excellent sound quality in production and cassette reproduction allows the subtle tones within the sound of the gong to emerge and shimmer.

KUTHUMI

Joel Andrews
Joel Andrews, 245 East Mountain Ave., Santa Barbara, CA 93108

entire album

The Ascended Master channeled powerfully in a solo harp meditation through Joel Andrews.

HYPERGNOSTIC MEDITATION

Arica
cassette #801, Arica Institute, 235 Park Ave. South, New York, N.Y. 10003

Hip, spacey, rhythmic movement meditation album.

MUSIQUE POUR LE REVE ET L'AMOUR (MUSIC FOR DREAM AND LOVE)

Ariel Kalma
SACEM A 888, Eurock Distributors, P. O. Box 4181, Torrance, CA 90510

RELATED MUSIC

SRI CHINMOY PLAYS THE ESRAJ

Sri Chinmoy
Sri Chinmoy Center, 2438 16th Avenue, San Francisco, CA 94116

ON MEDITATIVE MUSIC

Only the rarest forms of . . . music can maintain a flowing continuity, bring about a yielding introversion, extend an acoustic germcell like a mantra into infinity. Only a few products of this kind have the shape and the power, not to lead the listener into insensibility, but to evoke a contemplative self-absorption.

With meditation now very much a la mode, the concept of 'meditative music' is as yet ill-defined, and . . . it soon becomes obvious that any slow, gentle music is immediately dubbed 'meditative.' The concept has been made fun of, primarily by those who have never meditated in their lives, and who link meditation with all sorts of vague notions: drugs, hashish, cosmos, ecstasy, trance. Electronic horror-noises and Buddhist mantra-settings are, for many, one and the same. No wonder that the confusion has arisen: most musicians are themselves not quite clear as to what 'meditative music' really is. Does it even exist?

If one knows how to meditate, and has the necessary patience to press forward into deep inner levels, one listens inwardly, and exterior sources of sound are scarcely perceived at all. He who meditates hears no music. Nonetheless music can provide a meditative point of departure, and in particular can remove one's inner restlessness in the initial stages, quieten the ceaseless reasoning and cogitating. Music can provide a ritual such as may be needed in the early stages to stop oneself running away and to enable one to become really still. Music can also serve as an aid and a tool for relaxation, concentration and the achievement of inner quietness.

Now most of the music which is today categorised as 'meditative' is merely a form of imagery recounting the musician's own spiritual experiences and visions, describing 'the universal consciousness, the cosmic joy' and eagerly using it as an occasion for subjective music — music which, to the 'uninitiated' outsider, can seem naive, rhetorical, intoxicated or just rubbish. And with a few exceptions the meditator — he who really sits and is still and silent — cannot 'use' this music anyway. The only exception would be an improvisatory or contemplative music which is not about meditation and the self and God at all . . . but which is itself capable of being a vehicle, energy-form and magic force for spiritual self-absorption, a music which has no predetermined, stylistic function to perform, but which flows endlessly and will not be listened to as one listens to Classical music — indeed, which is not there to be perceived at all, but which works by virtue of its own inner laws, as soon as the listener learns how to open himself totally to it. It carries him away — to himself."

Peter Michael Hamel, Through Music to the Self

MUSIC FOR MEDITATION

Ali Akbar Khan
Connoisseur Society CS-2063

Bilaskhani Todi (alap)

An alap in 15 parts by the master of the sarod.

RAGA BHUPALI: SACHDEV IN CONCERT

G.S. Sachdev
Unity Records UR-600

side 1 (alap)

North Indian evening raga, sensitively rendered by a master of the Indian bamboo flute.

SARANGI/ THE VOICE OF A HUNDRED COLORS

Ram Narayan
Nonesuch Explorer H-72030

Nand-Kedar

Beautiful and deeply meditative raga by one of the foremost virtuosi of the sarangi, an Indian microtonal cello.

A BELL RINGING IN THE EMPTY SKY

Goro Yamaguchi
Nonesuch H-72025

Koku-Reibo (Bell Ringing in the Empty Sky), Sokaku-Reibo (Depicting the Cranes in Their Nest)

Great beauty and purity of traditional Japanese religious music. It is said that a single note of the shakuhachi can lead one directly into Nirvana.

RAG YAMAN KALYAN

Pandit Pran Nath
Shandar SR 10 007

This Indian master singer has had a great influence on several well-known American avant garde musicians, especially Terry Riley and LaMonte Young. His powerful singing represents the deepest traditions in Indian classical music.

JAVANESE COURT GAMELAN VOL. II

Nonesuch Explorer H-72074

Gending Bonang Babar Layar

Slow, regal, deep-toned gamelan piece.

BANSURI: THE INDIAN FLUTE

G. S. Sachdev
Phillips 6405 611

Early album recorded in India. Traditional raga— flute, tamboura and tabla.

YOGA

Popul Vuh
Cosmic Couriers pld. SQ-6606

Real Indian music by Indian musicians, excellently recorded in Germany by the leader of Popol Vuh.

THE DAGAR BROTHERS: TWO RAGAS

Dagar Brothers
Musicaphon BM 30L-2018

Raga Asavari, Raga Bhairavi

Two really fabulous Indian singers.

*For Indian music, as for the performer himself, it is much more important that the public **should be able to listen with the heart,** rather than observe the musical development or 'appreciate' the music critically and dispassionately. In the West this attitude is commonly confused with 'emotionalism' and much pompous misrepresentation is associated with it. This 'listening with the heart' is nevertheless a very aware condition requiring both receptivity and the faculty of conscious, discriminating perception.*

Peter Michael Hamel

WORLD FUSION MUSIC

The evolving synthesis—in form and instrumentation—of Western and traditional world musics.

TIBETAN BELLS I

Henry Wolff and Nancy Hennings
Island SMAS-9317

entire album, especially A Choir of Bells

The original creative rediscovery of the bells by Western artists. Certainly a classic with timeless excellence. "It is the sound of the void." — H. H. Karmapa, Sikkim.

TIBETAN BELLS II

Henry Wolff and Nancy Hennings
Celestial Harmonies 006

Journey to the End, The Endless Journey (entire album)

Some of the highest sounds that can be brought onto the physical plane. Produced with great depth of understanding, this album actually improves upon its predecessor. A complete metaphysical journey. Very highly recommended.

DHARANA

Between
Wergo SM-1011

Om Namo Buddhaya, Listen to the Light, Sunset, Dharana

Dharana means deepest inner collection and concentration. The third album from Peter Michael Hamel and Between, in conjunction with a symphony orchestra, it is haunting and evocative of the delicate ether sounds of the spheres and massive sounds of the earth. Recommended.

NIGHT MUSIC

William Maraldo
unpublished tape

entire work

Entrancing Indian/electronic fusion improvised around 1970 by musicians collected in the San Francisco Bay Area, including Terry Riley, Jordan Stenberg (de la Sierra) and others.

RAGA MALCONCHE

Tantric Research Institute
unpublished tape

Live recording of a 1973 Berkeley concert of an ensemble of young Western musicians playing a beautiful fusion of Indian raga and Western improvisation.

FLOATING WORLDS

Future Primitives
Chin Hua Music, 2503 24th St., San Francisco 94110

The Emerald Mermaid's Reflection, Cloud Script, The Night Sky in October

Exotic and beautiful compositions for cheng, zither, sitar, sarangi, bowed vioella, flutes, voice.

AMAZING GRACE

Amazing Grace
unpublished tape

Tamboura Meditation

Very deep meditation for two large tambouras played by members of this now dispersed group. An amazing and powerful sound.

IF MAN BUT KNEW

The Habibiyya
Island SW-9395

Two Shakuhachis, Koto Piece, Mandola

Western Sufis playing and singing Eastern influenced music — "the heart's journey to the heart of the heart." Recently reissued.

SONG OF THE SEASHORE

James Galway
RCA ARL-13534

Virtuoso Western flautist meets Japanese string orchestra to produce this album of traditional and popular Japanese melodies. A bit oversweet in places but mostly just wonderful.

Those contemporary musicians and explorers of the inner world that have incorporated mystical-magical, spiritual, and metaphysical elements in their music . . . have contributed considerably to the integrative encounter with the Far East and to the shedding of acoustic light on man's esoteric knowledge. They could be the founding fathers of an entirely new form of world-music, now in its earliest infancy.

Peter Michael Hamel

VISIONS OF A PEACEFUL PLANET

Ancient Future
Ancient Future, 12 Maple Ave., Kentfield, CA 94904

Zzaj

A good record by a Marin County acoustic group — drawn mostly on Indian, Balinese and jazz influences. Our thanks to Ancient Future's principal musicians, Mindy Klein and Matthew Montfort, for creating the term, "world fusion music."

COSMIC CONSCIOUSNESS: PAUL HORN IN KASHMIR

Paul Horn
World Pacific WPS-21445

Raga Kerwani

Recorded in India with Indian virtuoso soloists.

DREAM SUITE

Light Rain
Magi 002; Magi, P. O. Box 356, Larkspur, CA 94939

Sundown Silhouette

California/Middle Eastern dance music. Undulate your way to total bliss. A great group.

PERSIAN SONGS

Minoo Javan
JEI, 2040 Avenue of the Stars, Suite 400, Los Angeles, CA 90067

Shir Ali Mardan, Nesa Nesa, Dokhtare Boyer Ahmadi

Persian romantic music with orchestral settings. Minoo Javan's voice will affect you. "The Judy Collins of Iran."

SPRING FLOWERS

Vasant Rai
Vanguard VSD-79379

Leaving Home

Jazz/Indian fusion by a fine Indian musician playing with members of Oregon.

DIGA

Diga Rhythm Band
United Artists RX-LA600-G/RX-110

Magnificent Sevens

A unique album if you can find it. Mickey Hart of the Grateful Dead produced and recorded an ensemble of virtually all of the virtuoso Indian/American drummers and percussionists in the Bay Area, with contributions by Jerry Garcia on guitar. Happiness is Drumming says it all. Beautiful cover art by Jordan de la Sierra.

THE RADHA KRSHNA TEMPLE

The Radha Krshna Temple, London
Apple SKAO-4476

Govinda

Mantra folk-rock, produced by George Harrison. A classic that wears well.

HEALING SOUNDS

Dr. Christopher Hills and the University of the Trees Choir
CH 24, University of the Trees Press, P. O. Box 644, Boulder Creek, CA 95006

Side 1, Srutis

Srutis are high frequency harmonics to certain sounds with profound effects on consciousness and the power, it is said, to disperse blockages in the energy system. This is a tape of srutis which appear ringing over the chanting of the University of the Trees Choir.

A MEDITATION MASS

Yatha Sidra
Brain Metronome 1045 (probably out of print)

Part I

German space-rock/Eastern dance music.

HEAR TO ETERNITY

Steven Jason Halpern
HS 793, Halpern Sounds, 620 Taylor Way, #14, Belmont, CA 94002

Sahara Sunrise, Incan Connection, Moonlight on the Ganges, Eternal Choir, Invocation, From Morocco to Benares, Oasis, Desert Wing

Steven Halpern uses ancient and electronic instruments to reproduce timeless consciousness-altering sounds — from the past, the present and the future — threaded together with Moroccan flute. The first four selections, evocative and mysterious, could well be called Contemporary Ancient

RELATED MUSIC

DO'A: ORNAMENT OF HOPE

Ken La Roche, Randy Armstrong
Philo 900, Philo Records, The Barn, N. Ferrisburg, VT 05473

DO'A: LIGHT UPON LIGHT

Philo 1056, Philo Records, The Barn, N. Ferrisburg, VT 05473

DAS HOHELIED SALOMOS (SACRED SONGS OF SOLOMON)

Popul Vuh
United Artists UAS 29-7811
Du Schönste der Wieber, Du Solem Davids I

There are musicologists in the East who are . . . telling me interesting things about how the grid of the Balinese gamelan — the tuning of their instruments — is, in a way, a mirror image of the tonality of Western music . . . They are playing what in our culture is left as the spaces.

Lawrence Blair

NEW AGE

We use this phrase only to describe contemporary songs whose lyrics contain New Age philosophy or concepts.

ROOTS AND WINGS

Sande Hershman

Roots and Wings, 234 Hawthorne, Larkspur, CA 94939

Blessed, Dream Song

Sande's voice is truly angelic. Blessed is one of the most beautiful "new age" songs out so far.

THE SUFI CHOIR

The Sufi Choir

Akashic Records; Sufi Islamia Ruhaniat Society, 410 Precita Ave., San Francisco, CA 94110

23rd Psalm

First album by the original Sufi Choir, containing some joyful, celebratory music. 23rd Psalm bursts into dance.

CRYIN' FOR JOY

The Sufi Choir

Sufi Islamia Ruhaniat Society, 410 Precita Ave., San Francisco, CA 94110

The Soul's Song to Itself, Gone

Evocative, original songs of the heart, creatively arranged by Allaudin Mathieu.

SWAHA

Bhagavan Das & Amazing Grace

c/o Hanuman Tape Library, Box 61498, Santa Cruz, CA 95061

Mother Song, Born on the Wings of a Dove, Blazing My Heart, Yah Devi, Let My Heart Fly Open

Devotional folk: great heartpourings of song by Western devotees of Neem Karoli Baba. Indian music influences.

Musicians are focalizers for a highly concentrated form of energy, an energy which affects those who experience the music on many levels of being. As we attune to unconditional love, to our highest Self, to the indwelling Spirit, this becomes the level upon which our music is based. As we become clearer channels of inner harmony, our intention for peace is extended through our music, and through our relations with each other. The spirit of cooperation replaces the need for competition as we come into balance with ourselves, and our music reflects how we feel about ourselves. The New Age is experienced in the presence of such musicians, and upon listening to such music.

Maitreya Stillwater

*We really are at a multidimensional crossroads. Sometimes at those moments when you don't know what to do with the situation in the world, when you can't see your way out, when it doesn't make any sense, when I say, what can I really do in the face of all this? – Well, I can sing. And I can perhaps encourage other people to sing. People together focusing their energy in that way, singing words that are affirming the positive, is an act of creation. The voice is a tool of creation. The words that we speak, the words that we sing, the thoughts that we have, **do** have an effect on the world.*

Sande Hershman

AN ALBUM OF ORIGINAL MUSIC

Dennis Wilcox
Goldust LPS-163

Snow on a Mountain, It's All the Same

Poetic, reflective songs of the spiritual search by folksinger Dennis Wilcox.

SEEDS OF PEACE

Stephen Longfellow Fiske
Fiske Music, 635 California Ave., Venice, CA 90291

Beethoven Raga

A fine debut album from a veteran singer/ songwriter from California New Age circles.

WINDS OF BIRTH

The New Troubadours
The Lorian Association, P. O. Box 1095, Elgin, Il 60120

The River, Canticle

Songs inspired by the cosmic and interpersonal energies of the Findhorn Community in Scotland. New Age philosopher David Spangler collaborated on the lyrics and sings in the group.

SONS OF THE 10TH GURU

The Khalsa String Band
NR-4108

O Guru Ram Das, Flowers in the Rain

Lyrical devotional songs by disciples of Yogi Bhajan.

STONE IN THE SKY

The Sufi Choir
Sufi Islamia Ruhaniat Society, 410 Precita Ave., San Francisco, CA 94110

Stone in the Sky

Light and high, a good song to start the day with.

ALL I SEE IS YOU

Rabindra Danks
Takoma/Devi D-1036

Lord, Lord, Lord; Lord's Sweet Name

One of the most professional sounding devotional albums by a veteran (originally Scottish) singer/ songwriter. Way too hip for 1973. Really excellent recording and music, produced by John Fahey.

Yet with the woes of sin and strife
The world has suffered long;
Beneath the heav'nly strain have rolled
Two thousand years of wrong;
And man, at war with man, hears not
The tidings which they bring;
O hush the noise, ye men of strife
And hear the angels sing.

For lo! the days are hast'ning on,
By prophets seen of old,
When with the ever-circling years
Shall come the time foretold,
When peace shall over all the earth
Its ancient splendors fling,
And the whole world give back the song
Which now the angels sing.

***It Came Upon a Midnight Clear,** Edmund H. Sears, 1846*

RELATED MUSIC

EVENING SONG

Marcus Allen, Bobbin Zahner & Peter Dupont
WA-102, Whatever Publishing, 158 E. Blithedale,
Suite 4, Mill Valley, CA 94941

SEEDS/HYMNS FOR A NEW AGE

Marcus Allen & Summer Raven
Whatever WA-101, Whatever Publishing, 158 E.
Blithedale, Suite 4, Mill Valley, CA 94941
Prayer in a Dream

WINGS OF PRAYER

Maitreya Stillwater
Heavensong, Box 605, Corte Madera, CA 94925
(cassette)

ONENESS SPACE

Love Band
Living Love-1
Sweet Surrender

SET YOUR HEARTSONG FREE

Maitreya Stillwater
Heavensong, Box 605, Corte Madera, CA 94925
(cassette)

AWAKENING

Heng Yin
Wondrous Sound Music, City of Ten Thousand
Buddhas, Box 217, Talmage, CA 95481

FULL MOON LIGHT

Sky Sulamyth
7th Ray Productions, P. O. Box 3771, Hollywood, CA
90028

Expanded-consciousness, though musically traditional folk songs not about freight trains, farming or da blooz.

CIRCLES IN THE STREAM

Bruce Cockburn
High Romance Music ILT9475

entire album

A double live album of Bruce Cockburn in concert. This wonderfully sensitive Canadian Christian/earth mystic is one of the most sophisticated artists in the area of folk/jazz chamber music. A great record start to finish with most of his best songs.

HIGH WINDS, WHITE SKY

Bruce Cockburn
True North TN 3

Let Us Go Laughing, Love Song, One Day I Walk, High Winds/White Sky, You Point to the Sky, Shining Mountain

Fresh, simple and beautiful album.

TRUE NORTH

Bruce Cockburn
Epic E-30812

Thirteenth Mountain, Spring Song

From a simple early album, these deep and poetic lines:
"Is only Man seeking one love
Searching vainly for excuse
among the stars above
Eyes too tired to see
The rivers flowing 'neath the ice
And too numb to see the purpose
behind knowing . . ."

TELLURIAN LULLABYE

Buddy Comfort
In production

With Love, Angels in Embryo, Galadriel

Long-awaited album from this excellent musician and superior singer, a twentieth century balladeer whose work is described as mellow baroque-folk with an infusion of jazz, North Indian and medieval. Buddy Comfort is a refined soul and a radiant heart, whose songs touch deeply.

Playing your music in starlight
Weaving these words like a dream
Drinking from the cup of your sweet, sweet eyes
O Mystery Lady, how you sing!

Your vina sings such a sweet sound
To my heart in tune with your song
Lover of my life, O Music, come down
Draw me for loving to you . . .

Music, sweet Music, come take me
Flying so high on your love
Winged bright angel of beauty
One guide, one light, from above. . . .

Usman Friedman
Sung by Buddy Comfort

RENAISSANCE OF THE CELTIC HARP

Alan Stivell
Polydor 2424 069

entire album, especially Ys and Marv Pontkalleg

A beautiful, fluid instrument with great expressive potential. Traditional songs, rendered beautifully. A classic.

THEME FROM
'THE LIGHT OF EXPERIENCE'

Gheorghe Zamfir
Epic EDC-81638

Theme from 'The Light of Experience'

Virtuoso pan-pipist Zamfir overflowing with sweet, slightly sad, longing. The rest of the selections are outrageously joyful dances.

ICE FLOWERS MELTING

Sylvan Grey
Kantele Recording, P.O. Box 655, Larkspur, CA 94939

Original improvisation on the Finnish kantele (folk harp), a sound that is precarious, crystal-like, meditative.

RELATED MUSIC

REFLETS

Alan Stivell
Fontana 6325-340
Suite des Montagnes, Marig ar Pollanton, Broceliande

SUNWHEEL DANCE

Bruce Cockburn
Epic KE-31768
Sunwheel Dance, Life Will Open, It's Going Down Slow

FINGERS AKIMBO

Michael Stenwood, Bruce Bowers
Biscuit City BC 1319
The Buttonwillow

SPIRITUAL POP

Contemporary popular songs which directly or indirectly speak of spiritual or religious experience.

HEART FOOD

Judee Sill
Asylum SD-5063

The Kiss, The Pearl, The Donor

An excellent and now out-of-print album composed, produced, arranged and performed by Judee Sill. The poetry of the lyrics continues to unfold after years of listening.

JUDEE SILL

Judee Sill
Asylum SD 5050 (out of print)

Crayon Angels, Lady-O, Lopin' Along Through the Cosmos, Abracadabra

Multitalented woman who writes, arranges, conducts and sings the songs on this album. Worth buying if you see it.

JUDY MAYHAN

Judy Mayhan
Decca DL 75287 (out of print)

Freest Fancy, I've Been the One, Mythical Kings and Iguanas, Dolphins, Sweet Reason, He Gives Us All His Love

As with her first album, if you see it in a used record bin, buy it. That depth of emotion and experience is rarely so subtly expressed in a voice.

MOMENTS

Judy Mayhan
ATCC SD 33-319 (out of print)

Shinin', Dream Goin' By, Begin Again, I Shall be Released

Extraordinary woman whose voice contains ages. Wonderful album, sadly out of print.

ILLUMINATIONS

Buffy St. Marie
Vanguard VSD-79300

God Is Alive/Magic is Afoot, The Angel, Poppies

Good album. The Angel is very wise. Excellent early use of electronic music techniques in pop songs.

FACES

Shawn Phillips
A&M 4363

L'Ballade

A Hearts of Space standard. Still beautiful after years of playings.

WATER BEARER

Sally Oldfield
Chrysalis 1121

entire album

A mythic concept album loosely based on J.R.R. Tolkien's Ring Trilogy, remarkable in the complexity and breadth of allusion and in the virtuosity of instrumentation and arrangement. Produced and performed by Sally Oldfield. And you can dance to it.

PHOENIX

Dan Fogelberg
Epic FE 35634

Along the Road

An especially fine album throughout from this gifted popular singer/songwriter contains this beauty.

Music attracts the angels in the universe.

Bob Dylan

MOONSHOT

Buffy St. Marie
Vanguard VSD-79312

Moonshot

Moonshot is a good alternative to the space program — one of the best songs about inner space travel.

CHANGING WOMAN

Buffy St. Marie
MCA 451

Eagle Man/Changing Woman, Nobody Will Ever Know It's Real But You

As always, sensitive, perceptive, with a few spacey romantic gems.

IT'S IN EVERYONE OF US

David Pomerantz
Arista AL 4053

It's in Every One of Us

A musically excellent album by this underrated artist with lyrics grounded in human potential philosophy. It's in Every One of Us has become somewhat of a banner song of that movement.

ESSENCE TO ESSENCE

Donovan
Epic KE-32800

There is an Ocean, The Dignity of Man, The Divine Daze of Deathless Delight, Sailing Homeward

Essence of the '60s vision, pure of heart. Good music. This was Donovan's long-awaited "spiritual" album. It was too late, but it's great that he did it.

SHORT STORIES

Vangelis/Jon Anderson
Polydor Deluxe, POLD 5030

I Hear You Now, The Road, Love Is, One More Time, A Play Within a Play

A perfect collaboration — songs by Jon Anderson of YES, music and orchestrations by Vangelis. Superb.

ALL THINGS MUST PASS

George Harrison
Apple STCH 639

Beware of Darkness

A most affecting song from George Harrison's first overtly "spiritual" album.

LIVING IN THE MATERIAL WORLD

George Harrison
Apple SMAS-3410

Be Here Now, That Is All

Two more good ones.

STORMBRINGER!

John and Beverly Martyn
Warner Bros. WS-1854

The Ocean

English folk/rock duo from early Donovan era with a very excellent album.

RESOLUTION

Andy Pratt
Nemperor NE 438

Some Things Go On Forever

Excellent album by an aware writer on the subject of growth and relationships.

POUR DOWN LIKE SILVER

Richard & Linda Thompson
Island ILPS-9348

Night Comes In, Dimming of the Day

English folk/rock duo.

WHALES AND NIGHTINGALES

Judy Collins
Elektra EKS 75010

Amazing Grace,   Nightingale II

Amazing Grace, a capella and with choir, is one of the most moving versions of the hymn.

GOODBYE YELLOW BRICK ROAD

Elton John
MC2-10003s

I've Seen That Movie Too

A cosmic ballad from the mature Elton John.

STEVIE WONDER'S JOURNEY THROUGH THE SECRET LIFE OF PLANTS

Stevie Wonder
Tamla T13-371C2

The Secret Life of Plants, Ecclesiastes

Such a good album! Stevie Wonder is a gift.

SIDDHA: A VERY GENTLE FORCE

Siddha
Julasi Manjari Record Co., P.O. Box 745, Corte Madera, CA 94925

Lovely One

Vision of Krishna . . . dreamlike . . . offered gently. Beautifully produced.

COMMON ONE

Van Morrison
Warner Bros., BSK-3462

When Heart Is Open

Another wonderful album in the fascinating, unfolding mystic journey of this great popular artist.

RELATED MUSIC

MAGICIANS

Jesse Morrow
unpublished demo album

Magicians

WHITE ROCK

Rick Wakeman
A&M SP-4614
The Loser

PRIMORDIAL LOVERS

Essra Mohawk
Reprise 6377
Looking Forward to the Dawn

CHI COLTRANE

Chi Coltrane
Columbia KC 31275
The Wheel of Life

BACK ROADS

Kate Wolf & The Wildwood Flower
Owl Records OL-001
The Redtail Hawk, Back Roads

"Come take my hand
You should know me
I've always been in your mind
You know I will be kind
I'll be guiding you . . .

From where I stand
You are home free
The planet's aligned so rare
There's promise in the air
And I'm guiding you . . .

REFUGEES

Rachel Faro
RCA CP-0689
Time Passes Slowly, Amazing Grace

LOVING AND FREE

Kiki Dee
MCA 395
Loving and Free

SING CHILDREN SING

Lesley Duncan
Columbia C-30663
Sing Children Sing, Love Song

INNERVISIONS

Stevie Wonder
Tamla T326L
Visions

ELTON JOHN

Elton John
DJM Records DJLPS 406
I Need You to Turn To

GHOSTS

Strawbs
A&M SP-4506
Starshine/Angel Wine

WHO CAME FIRST

Peter Townshend
MCA DL-79189
Content, Parvardigar

SURF'S UP

The Beach Boys
Brother Records (Warner Bros. Dist.) RS-6453
Feel Flows

FULFILLINGNESS FIRST FINALE

Stevie Wonder
Tamla T6 332S1
Heaven is 10 Zillion Light Years Away

A SONG FOR YOU

Bill Medley
A&M SP-3505
A Song for You, Somewhere, The Long and Winding Road

You have to believe we are magic
Nothing can stand in our way
You have to believe we are magic
Don't let your aim ever stray
And if all your heart survive
Destiny will arrive
And bring all your dreams alive
For you."

Magic, *John Farrar*
Sung by Olivia Newton-John

SEVENTH SOJOURN

Moody Blues
Threshold THS-7
New Horizons, Land of Make Believe

TEA FOR THE TILLERMAN

Cat Stevens
A&M SP-4280
Into White, Morning Has Broken

BUDDHA AND THE CHOCOLATE BOX

Cat Stevens
A&M SP-3623
Oh Very Young

THE BEST OF DONOVAN

Donovan
Hickory LPS-149
Catch the Wind

CATCH BULL AT FOUR

Cat Stevens
A&M SP-4365
Silent Sunlight

IMAGINE

John Lennon
Apple SW-3379
Imagine

MOONDANCE

Van Morrison
Warner Bros. 1835
Into the Mystic

SPIRIT

John Denver
RCA APL 1 1694
The Wings that Fly Us Home

LET IT BE

Beatles
Apple AR 34001
Across the Universe, Let It Be

THE DREAM WEAVER

Gary Wright
Warner Bros. BS-2868
Dream Weaver

Everything you do is music
And everywhere is the best seat.

–John Cage

HOME FREE

Dan Fogelberg
Columbia KC-31751
To the Morning

FLEETWOOD MAC

Fleetwood Mac
Warner Bros. MS-2225
Crystal

IN THE FALLING DARK

Bruce Cockburn
True North ILTN-9463 (dist. by Island)
In the Falling Dark, Lord of the Starfields

SGT. PEPPER'S
LONELY HEARTS CLUB BAND

Beatles
Capitol SMAS-2653
Within You/Without You

L'HEPTADE

Harmonium
Le Cinq Saison

SHINE ON BRIGHTLY

Procol Harum
A&M 4151
In Held T'was I

MUSIC FROM BIG PINK

The Band
Capitol SIC-AO 2955
I Shall Be Released

SUNSHINE SUPERMAN

Donovan
Epic BN 26217
Guinevere, Legend of a Girl Child Linda

ENDLESS FLIGHT

Leo Sayer
Warner Bros. BS-2962
Endless Flight, When I Need You

THE VELVET UNDERGROUND

The Velvet Underground
MGM SE-4617
Jesus

SLOW TRAIN COMING

Bob Dylan
CBS FC 36120
When He Returns, Do Right, Baby, (Do Unto Others),
When You Goin' to Wake Up?, Man Gave Names to
All the Animals, I Believe in You, Slow Train Comin

TUSK

Fleetwood Mac
Warner Bros. 2HS 3350
Storms, Sarah

BLUE AQUARIUS

Blue Aquarius
Gospel Truth GTS-2725 (out of print)
At the Feet of the Master

ON THE THRESHOLD OF A DREAM

Moody Blues
London DES-18025
The Voyage

JONATHAN LIVINGSTON SEAGULL

Neil Diamond
Columbia JS-32550
Hymn (edited)

PATRICK MORAZ

Patrick Moraz
Atlantic SD-18175
Best Years of Our Lives

SANDY

Sandy Denny
A&M SP-4371
Quiet Joys of Brotherhood, It'll Take a Long Time

FULL SAIL

Loggins & Messina
Columbia KC-32540
Pathway to Glory, Sailin' the Wind

TRANSCENDENCE

Shawn Phillips
RCA AFL 1-3028
Ease Your Mind, Motes of Dust

COSMIC ROCK

MEDDLE

Pink Floyd
Harvest SMAS-832

Echoes (last 1/2)

A great track from one of this group's best albums.

THE DARK SIDE OF THE MOON

Pink Floyd
SMAS-11163

Us and Them

Classic Pink Floyd and one of the biggest rock albums ever. Great sound by Alan Parsons.

WISH YOU WERE HERE

Pink Floyd
Columbia PC-33453

Shine on You Crazy Diamond I-VII

Supposedly Pink Floyd's tribute to original member Syd Barrett, now in service on other planes. Consistently good music in their mature style.

CORRELATIONS

Ashra (Manuel Gottsching, Harald Grosskopf, Lutz Ulbrich)
Virgin V2117

Morgana da Capo

German space band with a developed electronic rock style.

BLACKOUTS

Ashra
Virgin 25686-XOT

Blackouts, 77 Slightly Delayed

More speedy, enjoyable, disposable spacerock from Manuel and the boys.

GO

Stomu Yamashta, Steve Winwood, Michael Shrieve and Klaus Schulze
Island ILPS-9387

Side A all except Man of Leo

Japanese composer/percussionist attempts a space-rock concept album with generally excellent results. Vocals by Steve Winwood, synthesizers by Klaus Schulze.

WHO WILL SAVE THE WORLD? . . . THE MIGHTY GROUNDHOGS

Groundhogs
United Artists UAS-5570

Amazing Grace

An amazing Amazing Grace, funky and beautiful for organ and electric guitar.

SPACE ODDITY

David Bowie
RCA LSP-4813
Space Oddity

Great early album with this lost ozone space classic:
"Ground control to Major Tom . . ."

OLIAS OF SUNHILLOW

Jon Anderson
Atlantic SD-18180

Song of Search, Ocean Song

Fantasy concept album by YES vocalist Jon Anderson.

SOLAR FIRE

Manfred Mann's Earth Band
Polydor PD-6019

Father of Day/Father of Night

An album of Dylan songs reverently re-created in a powerful cosmic rock style.

RELATED MUSIC

AGES

Edgar Froese
Virgin VD-2507
Tropic of Capricorn

ALONE TOGETHER

Dave Mason
Blue Thumb Records BTS-19
World in Changes

ONE OF THESE NIGHTS

Eagles
Asylum 7E-1039
Take It to the Limit

BLIND FAITH

Eric Clapton, Steve Winwood, Ginger Baker, Rick Grech
Atco SD33-3048
Presence of the Lord, Can't Find My Way Home

FOR YOUR PLEASURE . . .
THE SECOND ROXY MUSIC ALBUM

Bryan Ferry, Andrew Mackay, Eno, et al.
E.G.Records (Warner Bros.) BS-2696
Strictly Confidential

VOLUNTEERS

Jefferson Airplane
RCA L-4238
Good Shepherd

ELDORADO

Electric Light Orchestra
United Artist UA-LA-339-G
Can't Get It Out of My Head

A NEW WORLD RECORD

Electric Light Orchestra
Jet JZ-35529
Tightrope, Mission, Above the Clouds

SAILOR

Steve Miller Band
Capitol ST-2984
Dear Mary

TO THE WORLD OF THE FUTURE

Earth & Fire
Polydor 2925-033

HERZ AUS GLAS

Popul Vuh
Brain 0060-079

NIPPON JIN:
JOIN OUR MENTAL PHASE SOUND

Far East Family Band
Vertigo 6370-850
The Cave

TENKUJIN

Far East Family Band
All Ears FE-11479

I ROBOT

Alan Parsons Project
Arista 7002

SPACE ART

Space Art (Dominique Perrier & Roger Rizzitelli)
If Records 67173

TRIP IN THE HEAD CENTER

Space Art
If Records 67213

JUMP ON IT

Montrose
Warner Bros. BS-2963
Music Man

DEAR MR. FANTASY

Traffic
United Artists LO-6657
Dealer

DREAM ON

Aerosmith
Columbia 3-10278
Dream On

JERRY GARCIA

Jerry Garcia
Warner Bros. BS-2582
To Lay Me Down

PSYCHEDELIC PROGRAM MUSIC

PINK FLOYD

Pink Floyd
Tower ST-5131

A Saucerful of Secrets (last 1/2), Set the Controls for the Heart of the Sun

Earliest psychedelic/electronic space Pink . . . Defines the term Psychedelic Program Music.

LIVE DEAD

The Grateful Dead
Warner Bros. 2WS-1830

Death Don't Have No Mercy, Dark Star

Experimental psychedelic electronic journeys from The Dead at the peak of their first period in 1970. Defines the term far-out.

ALPHA CENTAURI

Tangerine Dream
Brain 2/1082

Alpha Centauri

Vintage psychedelic period T-Dream. Amazing then and now.

ZEIT

Tangerine Dream
OHR OMM 2/56021

Nebulous Dawn, Origin of Supernatural Probabilities, Birth of Liquid Pleiades

Two-record set; spacey-trippy. Early psychedelic music by this pioneer German electronic band.

It is LSD which will be remembered as the sacrament of the Aquarian religion—the chemical channel for the visionary conversion of a whole generation. Music is the integrative ritual of this metanoia, the tapestry of harmony which bypasses the intellect and directly touches the feelings. The wordless music carries the listeners who submit to its power to the weightless area of pure experience, and they begin to resonate together, as an entire generation, not only to the same rhythm but to the same thought-patterns. Through its sheer volume the music of the '60s and '70s has served to soften the conditioned mind and also, with its lyrics, to seed it with the poetry of a new teaching . . . It speaks to an enormous and receptive public of fears and passions, of transcendent insights; it nurtures the feeling of other worlds in a language curiously alien to the traditional articulation of the sacred. In the music we have the movement into a new time, with the syncretism of archaic and heraldic symbolism with that of space-age technology.

*Lawrence Blair, **Rhythms of Vision*** 53

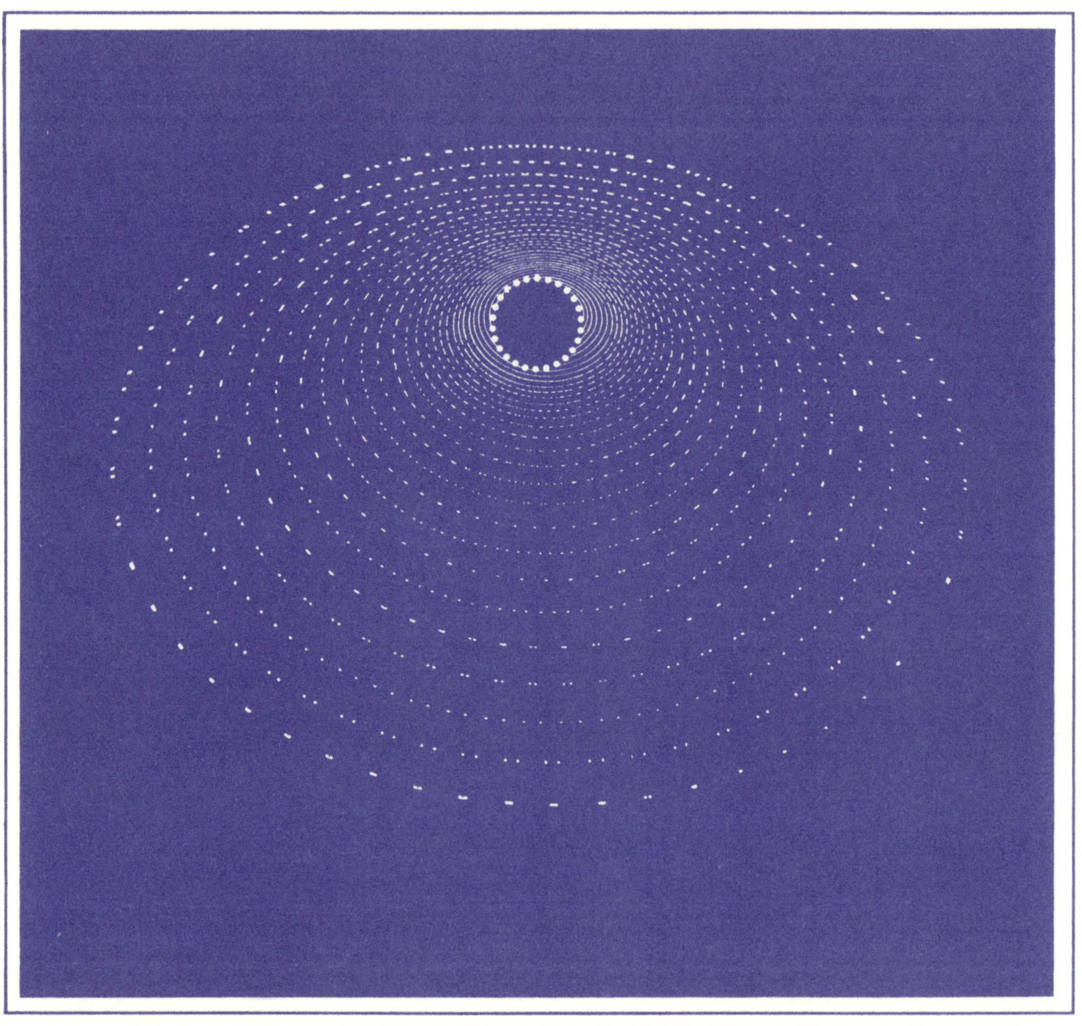

RELATED MUSIC

ZABRISKIE POINT

Jerry Garcia
MGM -4668ST
Love Scene

PROCOL HARUM

Procol Harum
Deram DES-18008
Whiter Shade of Pale

SURREALISTIC PILLOW

Jefferson Airplane
RCA LSP-3766
Comin Back to Me

PINK FLOYD

Pink Floyd
Tower ST-5093
The Gnome

ARBOUR ZENA

Keith Jarrett
ECM 1-1070

Runes (Dedicated to the Unknown)

A concerto for string orchestra, jazz ensemble and solo piano. Keith Jarrett as a classical composer. Truly excellent.

TIMELESS

John Abercrombie
ECM 1047/ST

Timeless, Love Song

Timeless, ageless piece of music — one of the best space jazz selections. Synthesizer and guitar.

PATHLESS PATH

Charles Lloyd
Unity Records UR 708

Pole Star, The Call, Pathless Path, Sea Angel, Agni

Lovely Japanese-inspired meditative jazz ensemble music. Excellent performances by all musicians involved. A very mature album which confirms a new chapter in Charles Lloyd's long career.

GANDHARVA

Beaver and Krause
Warner Bros. WS-1909

Gandharva, By Your Grace, Good Places, Short Film for David, Bright Shadows

A classical/jazz hybrid, with Moog synthesizer, cathedral organ and the 7 second reverberation of Grace Cathedral in San Francisco. Features Gerry Mulligan on saxophone, Gail Laughton's harp.

DISTANT HILLS

Oregon
Polydor VSD-79341

Distant Hills

A mature and excellent album by this well-known fusion group. Distant Hills evokes the California landscape for us.

ODYSSEY

Terje Rypdal
ECM-1067/68 ST

Adagio, Farewell, Ballade

Deep Nordic soul music which goes far beyond its jazz origins. Really classic contemporary chamber music. Very spacey.

AFTER THE RAIN

Terje Rypdal
ECM-1-1083

After the Rain, Little Bell, Like a Child/Like a Song; also Autumn Breeze, Air, Now and Then, Wind

Spacey, lyrical, sensual — excellent — jazz. The warmest album by far from this Nordic spaceman.

DESCENDRE

Terje Rypdal
ECM 1-1144

Speil, Avskjed, Descendre

This album from 1979 continues the wonderfully ecstatic spacey electronic guitar work of Terje's earlier records in an ensemble including trumpet, flugelhorn, drums and percussion, and electronic keyboards. The other tracks are marred (for us) by typically nervous jazz rhythm patterns, but Terje's guitar is always "edge of the edge."

No sound is dissonant which tells of life.

Coleridge

CALLINGS

The Paul Winter Consort
Living Music Records LMR-1 (2 record set)

all

Gentle, lovely music celebrating the sea and its creatures. The Consort, other musicians, and the voices of 13 sea mammals — California sea lion, harp seal, bearded seal, fur seal, sea otter, dolphin, blue whale, humpback whale, bowhead whale, beluga, orca, walrus, polar bear. High quality recording in The Cathedral of St. John the Divine, New York City.

LORD OF LORDS

Alice Coltrane
Impulse-9224

Going Home

A sparkling and alive version of the traditional American spiritual in an intensely romantic version for harp and string orchestra.

TRANSCENDENCE

Alice Coltrane
Warner Bros. BS 3077

Side 1

Deeply felt music, primarily for harp.

ALICE COLTRANE WITH STRINGS

Alice Coltrane
Impulse AS-9218

Galaxy in Satchidananda

''Love is a sacred word. Love is the name of God . . .'' — spoken by Swami Satchidananda to music of organ, harp, tamboura by Alice Coltrane.

SILENCE BEYOND TIME

Between
Wergo Spectrum SM 1023

Das Molekül, Silence Beyond Time, Peaceful Piece, Movens

1980 album by a European group who are comparable to the American group Oregon. Sophisticated jazz-based musicians who have absorbed and transformed the music of many cultures on the path to a new ''world fusion music.'' Peter Michael Hamel on keyboards.

COMMON GROUND

The Paul Winter Consort
A&M SP 4698

Ocean Dream, Lay Down Your Burden

The Consort's tribute to the cries of the whale, the wolf, and the great birds with the music they evoke. Very fine music, semi-adequate vocals.

SARGASSO SEA

John Abercrombie and Ralph Towner
ECM-1-1080

Fable, Sargasso Sea

Moving layers of shifting guitar textures by two jazz masters.

EAST WINDOW

East Window
Stephen Coughlin, 28A Edison Ave., Corte Madera, CA 94925

East Window, Rainbow Island, La Luz, Kyrie

Jazz with light. The devotional centering of Stephen Coughlin, reeds, and Moulabakhsh Funk, piano, is an invisible harmonic, very apparent vibrationally.

UPON REFLECTION

John Surman
ECM 1-1148

Edges of Illusion

Saxophonist and composer in a solo album of synthesizer/horn combinations. Influences range from Baroque music and jazz to Terry Riley with some enjoyable results.

SOLSTICE

Ralph Towner with Jan Garbarek, Eberhard Weber, Jon Christensen
ECM 1060

Drifting Petals

Aptly named; light, suggesting, ephemeral jazz images.

CLOSENESS

Charlie Hayden and Alice Coltrane
Horizon (A&M) SP-710

For Turia, Closeness

From an album of duets by Charlie Hayden and others, this one emerges. Extraordinary music for double bass and harp.

WEATHER REPORT

Weather Report
Columbia C-30661

Milky Way

Brief, crystalline flight to interspace from the first album by this popular avant group.

DIS

Jan Garbarek, Ralph Towner
ECM 1093

Viddene, Dis

Genuine icy Nordic soul/space music with synthesizer, wind harp, and the intense clear sound of Garbarek's flute and saxophone.

RELATED MUSIC

WAVES

Jade Warrior
Island ILPS-9318

FLOATING WORLD

Jade Warrior
Island ILPS-9290

WINTER LIGHT

Oregon
Vanguard VSD-79350
Deer Path

I SING THE BODY ELECTRIC

Weather Report
Columbia KC-31352
Crystal

BEYOND THE LONELIEST SEA

Peter Banks and Jan Akkerman
Capitol SMAS 11217

Music fathoms

the sky

Baudelaire

REFLECTIONS

Laura Allan
Unity Records UR 707

As I Am, Waterfall, Nicasio, Passage

An extraordinarily pure and beautiful voice, Laura Allan composes, sings, and plays zither on this long-awaited album, with flute accompaniment by Paul Horn. Highly recommended.

BIG SUR TAPESTRY

Charles Lloyd, with Georgia Kelly, harp
Pacific Arts PAC 7-139

Partington Cove, Partington Point, Hill of the Hawk

High and airy, side 1 is one of the loveliest flute experiences available.

YOU ARE THE OCEAN

Schawkie Roth
Center of Heavenly Music, P. O. Box 1063, Larkspur, CA 94939

Spanish Rivers, Inner Freedom, Rising Waves, You Are the Ocean

Flowing music of flute, zither, harp and cello for relaxation and massage. Many beautiful moments, especially Spanish Rivers.

TO THE ESSENCE OF A CANDLE

Larkin
Wind Sung Sounds, 1259 El Camino Real, Suite 9, Menlo Park, CA 94025

A Journey Through Bamboo, Silver Meditations

Pure, meditative solo flute music. Simple and effective.

INNER LIGHT OF LIFE

Akira Itoh
King SKS-38

Lush, romantic Japanese synthesizer music, verging on Easy Listening.

HEAVEN ON EARTH

Schawkie Roth
Center of Heavenly Music, P.O. Box 1063, Larkspur, CA 94939

Heaven on Earth

Joyful, fluid meditative piece for zither, flute, saxophone, voice and natural sounds.

AN ANGEL SINGS/AMBIENCE

Joel Andrews
Joel Andrews, 245 East Mountain Ave., Santa Barbara, CA 93108 (cassette)

Ambience

Intended to release love between two people, this is also a harmonious vibration to bathe in alone, allowing scattered parts of oneself to come into balance.

RAINBOW RAY OF THE MASTERS

Schawkie Roth, flute; Deborah Henson-Conant, harp
Center of Heavenly Music, P.O. Box 1063, Larkspur, CA 94939

Rainbow Ray of the Masters, Improvisation: To the One

Schawkie Roth's flute lifts and soars, Deborah Henson-Conant's harp is subtle and intricate on this latest release from Heavenly Music. The title song is especially lovely.

THE GOLDEN VOYAGE: VOLUMES I, II, III

Bearns and Dexter
Awakening Productions, 4132 Tuller Ave., Culver City, CA 90230

Relaxation/meditation voyages, loved by many and condemned by others as ''New Age'' musak. Nature ambiences, synthesizer, piano, bells, etc. Concentrates on resonating with higher musical, hence vibratory, frequencies.

RESTFUL AND RELAXING

Music consciously created to slow down, balance out and open up the body/mind.

*For those who do not love
music drives away hate.
Music gives peace to the restless,
and comforts the sorrowful.
They who no longer
know where to turn
find new ways,
and those who have despaired
gain new confidence and love.*

Pablo Casals

MUSIC FOR AN INNER JOURNEY, VOL. I

Steve Bergman
Steve Bergman, P. O. Box 4577, Carmel, CA 93921

Oriental Suite

Music for piano, flute, bass and synthesizer — light, with healing energies.

ARICA

The Arica Musicians
A1-1001-1 (published 1970; may be out of print)
Arica Institute, 235 Park Ave. South, New York, N.Y. 10003

Relaxation

A record to accompany the Arica training, with instructions for using the music to clear the body. Relaxation (5:35) takes you immediately into that state with gongs and bells.

ZODIAC SUITE

Steven Halpern
HS-771, Halpern Sounds, 620 Taylor Way, #14, Belmont, CA 94002

Moonrise Over Orion, The Heard Eye, Sky Boat Theme

Designed to provide an entry to the "I" within, with Steven Halpern on electric and grand piano, Tony Selvage, electric violin, and Schawkie Roth, zither, alto and bamboo flutes.

SPECTRUM SUITE

Steven Halpern
HS-770

entire album

Steven Halpern's first solo electric piano album relates the 7 keynotes of the musical octave and the 7 colors of the visual spectrum to the 7 chakras. Designed to be soothing and relaxing.

PRELUDE

Steven Halpern
HS-795 (cassette), Halpern Sounds, 620 Taylor Way, #14, Belmont, CA 94002

Awakening

Peaceful, expansive variations based on the traditional tamboura tuning at the root of Indian music.

BREATHE

Noj Bernoff, Marcus Allen
Whatever Publishing, 158 E. Blithedale, Suite 4, Mill Valley, CA 94941

Medieval Mist, Interlude, One Earth, Dance on the Wind, Breathe

Light and relaxing "New Age" sound for vibraphone, electric and acoustic space piano by two California musicians.

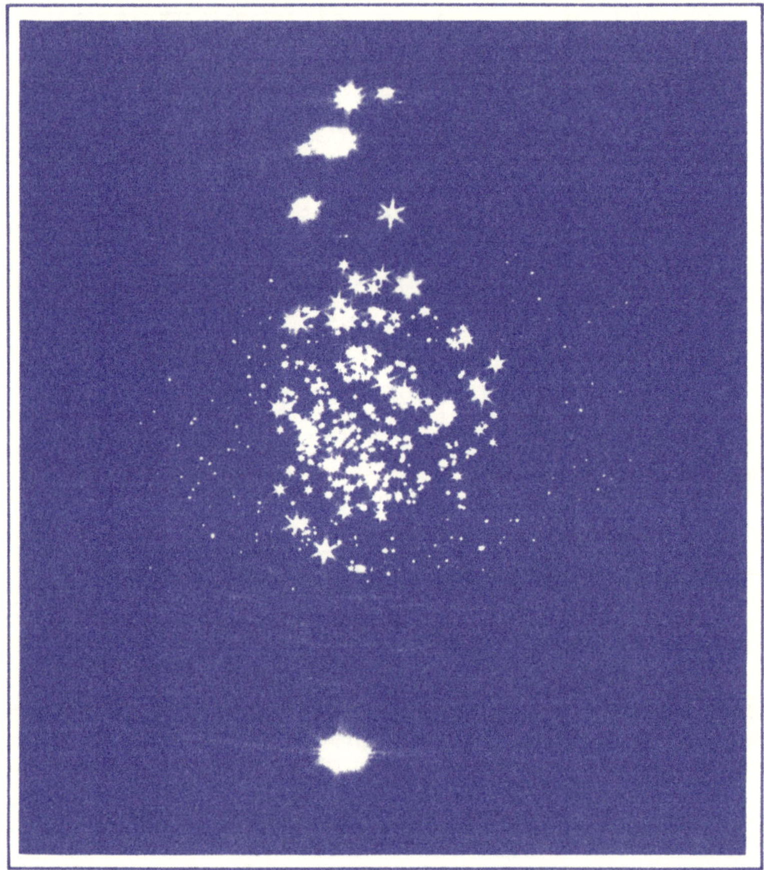

RELATED MUSIC

KANTELE

Marti Pokela
Finnlevy SF LP 8578

EASTERN PEACE

Steven Halpern
HS-782 (cassette), Halpern Sounds, 620 Taylor Way,
#14, Belmont, CA 94002

WATERFALL MUSIC:
CRYSTALS FOR SOLO PIANO

Paul Warner
Waterfall Music, Box 43, Kula, Maui, Hawaii 96790
(cassette)

STARBORN SUITE

Steven Halpern
HS-780 (cassette), Halpern Sounds, 620 Taylor Way,
#14, Belmont, CA 94002

STEVEN HALPERN "LIVE" IN CONCERT

Steven Halpern
HS-777 (cassette), Halpern Sounds, 620 Taylor Way,
#14, Belmont, CA 94002

MAHLER: SYMPHONY NO. 5 IN C SHARP

The Chicago Symphony/George Solti
London 2228

Adagietto

Graceful and emotional, this releases the heart.

HOVHANESS: MUSIC FOR TRUMPET AND ORGAN, OP. 200

Maurice Stith (trumpeter)
Redwood Records ES-2

Music for Trumpet and Organ, Op. 200

Part of a series of trumpet instructional records. Yearningly beautiful. Fine playing, excellent music.

RALPH VAUGHAN WILLIAMS: A LARK ASCENDING

The Philharmonia Orchestra/Sir Adrian Boult/ Hugh Bean, violin
Angel S-36469

A Lark Ascending

Lovely, soaring orchestral inspiration by this 20th century English composer. The solo violin flies beyond the heart.

BERNSTEIN CONDUCTS IVES

The New York Philharmonic/Leonard Bernstein
MS-6843

The Unanswered Question

Yearning, heartrending question. A very rare expression in music.

ADAGIO

Berlin Philharmonic/Herbert von Karajan
Deutsche Grammophon 2530 247

Albinoni: Adagio in G Minor for Strings and Organ

One of the major league adagios. This version is fabulous: poignant, with dignity.

JOAQUIN RODRIGO/NARCISO YEPES

Narciso Yepes, Orquesta Sinfonica R.T.V. Espana/ Odon Alonso
Deutsche Grammophon 139 440

Concierto de Aranjuez

Andalusian soul music — the essence of Spain. Versions by Andres Segovia and John Williams also recommended.

The musician's art is to send light into the depths of men's hearts.

Robert Schumann

The sounds proceeding from the instruments of symphonic music seem to be the very organs of the mysteries of creation; for they reveal, as it were, the primal stirrings of creation which brought order out of Chaos long before the human heart was there to behold them.

Richard Wagner

SEGOVIA

Andres Segovia
Decca DL 710027

Rodrigo: Fantasia para Gentilhombre (Adagio)

"Official" version for guitar and orchestra. See also James Galway's lovely flute/orchestra version.

JAMES GALWAY PLAYS RODRIGO

James Galway/Philharmonia Orchestra/ Eduardo Mata
RCA ARL 1-3416

Fantasia para Gentilhombre

The liquid, heart-filled quality of Galway's flute is the perfect complement to the rich sonorities of this wonderful contemporary Spanish music.

ALAN HOVHANESS: AVAK, THE HEALER/PRAYER OF ST. GREGORY

Crystal Chamber Orchestra/Ernest Gold/Marni Nixon, soprano/Thomas Stevens, trumpet
Crystal S 800

Avak, the Healer, Op. 65; Prayer of St. Gregory

Clear, high trumpet, pure soprano and strings in Avak, a Western classic work with echoes of Middle Eastern mystery traditions. In the Prayer of St. Gregory, Hovhaness again uses the trumpet as an instrument of aspiration and certainty, here to a background of lovely hymnal tones.

STOKOWSKI PLAYS BACH

Leopold Stokowski/London Symphony Orchestra
Seraphim S-60235

Komm, Süsser Tod; Passacaglia and Fugue in C Minor; Shepherd's Song (Christmas Oratorio)

Stowkowski in top form with superb orchestral transcriptions of these Bach classics.

BEETHOVEN PIANO SONATAS

Daniel Barenboim
Angel SNLV-3755-6

The Moonlight Sonata (Sonata #14 in C# Minor, Op. 27, No. 2, Adagio)

This movement of Beethoven's familiar sonata somehow remains above numerous attempts to defile it — simple and lovely.

MAHLER: DAS LIED VON DER ERDE

New York Philharmonic/Bruno Walter
Columbia MS-6426

Der Abschied (The Farewell)

Inspired by Chinese poems and the consciousness of his own approaching death, this is regarded by many as Mahler's greatest work — here conducted by his close friend, Bruno Walter.

LEONARD ROSE/EUGENE ORMANDY

**Leonard Rose/The Philadelphia Orchestra/
Eugene Ormandy**
Columbia M-30113

Faure: Elegie for Cello and Orchestra

Truly an elegy, with all its sadness and softness.

SONGS OF CATALONIA

**Victoria de los Angeles/Orquesta Civdad de
Barcelona**
Angel S-36682

Damont de tu Nomes les Flors, Canco de Seca

The clear voice of Victoria de los Angeles in the
sweet nostalgia of traditional Spanish songs.

ALAN HOVHANESS:
MAJNUN SYMPHONY

**John Alldis Choir/The National Philharmonic
Orchestra of London**
Poseidon 1016

The Celestial Beloved, The Mysterious Beloved

A symphony for chorus and orchestra based on the
story of Majnun and Layla, the Persian Romeo and
Juliet legend — the drama of love, attachment,
devotion and separation. Haunting, affecting music.

BACH: CONCERTO IN E MAJOR FOR VIOLIN AND STRING ORCHESTRA, CONCERTO IN A MINOR FOR VIOLIN AND STRING ORCHESTRA, CONCERTO IN D MINOR FOR TWO VIOLINS AND STRING ORCHESTRA

I Musici
Epic BC-1080

Masterful, warmly definitive recordings of these
great Baroque concerti by an Italian chamber
orchestra. The slow movements of each are
beautiful, but the adagio of the D Minor (for two
soloists) is music of the utmost yearning, beauty and
tenderness. "It was through this piece that I
discovered the music of the heart." — Timitheo.

IX. RESEARCH PERIOD, THE WORKS OF JOHANN SEBASTIAN BACH (SERIES F: ORGANWORKS)

Helmut Walcha
Archiv ARC-3205

Passacaglia in C Minor

One of Bach's greatest and most subtle
compositions for the organ — an austere version by
this blind German artist.

*When the great musicians wrote their wonderful music they turned in
unconscious remembrance towards that Cosmic pre-earthly existence from
out of which they were born for earthly life . . . It is as though they said, 'It is
human destiny, and rightly so, that man as he begins his earthly course of
life is placed into earthly conditions and must adapt himself to them. But in
his music he goes back again a little step; he leaves the earthly life to flow on
around him, and retreating for a moment draws near once more to the world
of soul and Spirit, the pre-earthly life from which he has come forth . . . He
steps back again for a moment into the Music of the Spheres.*

Rudolf Steiner 63

HOLST: THE PLANETS

Zubin Mehta/Los Angeles Philharmonic
London CS-6734

Neptune, The Mystic; Venus, The Bringer of Peace

Indubitably Western classical in form, these were nevertheless reachings toward the cosmic: Venus is interpreted in beauty, Neptune as a distant divinity.

CONCERTO FOR ONDES MARTENOT, STRINGS, ORCHESTRA AND PERCUSSION

Marcel Landowski
Musical Heritage Society MS-988-F

Adagio

Another discovery from the MHS treasurehouse — a concerto for (one of the earliest) synthesizers and orchestra.

THE POWER AND THE GLORY

Lloyd Holzgraf
M&K Real Time RT-114

Vivaldi: Largo (D Minor Concerto); Alexander Russell: The Bells of St. Anne de Beaupre

A direct-to-disc recording with bass which would all but disappear in broadcast, it is recommended for the two quiet organ works listed.

BLACK COMPOSERS SERIES, VOL. 7

The London Symphony Orchestra/Paul Freeman
Columbia M-33433

George Walker: Lyric for Strings

Lovely, emotional music with a hint of tragedy toward the end.

MESSIAEN: TURANGALILA SYMPHONY

Toronto Symphony/Seiji Ozawa/Jeanne Loriod, Ondes Martenot
RCA LSC-7051

VI. Jardin du sommeil d'amour (Garden of Love's Sleep)

We only play one movement from this otherwise dissonant sounding symphony. Features orchestra with electronic accompaniment from an early French synthesizer called the Ondes Martenot.

RELATED MUSIC

ROSEWOOD AND SILVER

Vance Koenig, classical guitar; Warren Weisbach, flute
privately published

Bach: Siciliano; Chopin: Prelude No. 4 in E Minor; Giuliani: Grand Sonata for Flute and Guitar, Op. 85; Beethoven: Moonlight Sonata

A collection of classical works, some adapted for flute and guitar, played with purity and gentleness.

LIGETI: REQUIEM, LONTANO, CONTINUUM

Gyorgy Ligeti
Wergo WER 60045
Lontano

BENJAMIN BRITTEN

Mstislav Rostropovich/The English Chamber Orchestra/Benjamin Britten
London 6419
Haydn: Concerto in C for Cello and Orchestra (Adagio)

To realize that we are one with the Creator as Beethoven did is a wonderful and awe-inspiring experience. Very few human beings ever come into that realization, and that is why there are so few great composers or creative geniuses . . . I always contemplate all this before commencing to compose. This is the first step. When I feel the urge I begin by appealing directly to my Maker . . . I immediately feel vibrations which thrill my whole being . . . In this exalted state I see clearly what is obscure in my ordinary moods; then I feel capable of drawing inspiration from above as Beethoven did . . . Those vibrations assume the form of distinct mental images . . . Straightaway the ideas flow in upon me, directly from God, and not only do I see distinct themes in the mind's eye, but they are clothed in the right forms, harmonies, and orchestration. Measure by measure the finished product is revealed to me when I am in those rare, inspired moods . . . I have to be in a semi-trance condition to get such results—a condition when the conscious mind is in temporary abeyance, and the subconscious is in control, for it is through the subconscious mind, which is a part of Omnipotence that the inspiration comes.

Johannes Brahms

HARP SOUNDINGS

Joel Andrews
Golden State Records LP-792, 665 Harrison St., San Francisco, CA

IVES: SYMPHONY NO. 4

Leopold Stokowski/American Symphony Orchestra
Columbia ML-6175
Largo maestoso

HARP AUJOURD'HUI

Marcella DeCray
Coronet 2745
Prokofieff: Prelude, Op. 12, No. 7

MUSIC FOR GLASS HARMONICA

Bruno Hoffman
VOX STDL 501.110
Mozart: Adagio in C, K.617a; Johann Abraham Peter Schulz: Largo in C Minor

HEAVY ORGAN AT CARNEGIE HALL

Virgil Fox
RCA ARDI-0081

VIRGIL FOX HEAVY ORGAN

Virgil Fox
DL-7-5323

OLIVIER MESSIAEN: VISIONS DE L'AMEN

Peter Serkin and Yuji Takahashi
RCA A-10363
Amen de la Creation

VIRGIL FOX PLAYS REUBKE, PIERNE AND BACH

Virgil Fox
HCR-1701-SD74
Reubke: Sonata in C Minor on the 94th Psalm (Adagio)

WESTERN SACRED

FAURE REQUIEM

Choir of Kings College/The New Philharmonia Orchestra/David Willcocks
Seraphim S-60096

entire work, especially Agnus Dei, In Paradisum

A beautiful rendering of one of the loveliest and softest of requiems.

BRAHMS: A GERMAN REQUIEM

New Philharmonic Chorus and Orchestra/Loren Maazel
Columbia MZ 34583

Selig sind, die da Leid tragen

Deep, moving and fluid; sweet and sad. One of the most profound and beautiful sacred choral works for us.

O GREAT MYSTERY, UNACCOMPANIED CHORAL MUSIC OF THE 16th & 17th CENTURIES

The Canby Singers
Nonesuch H-71026

Tomas Luis de Victoria: O Magnum Mysterium; Lassus: Resonet in Laudibus

Very good record. Includes the O Magnum Mysterium of Morales and Byrd as well.

HYMNS SPHERES

Keith Jarrett
ECM-2-1086

Hymn of Remembrance, Hymn of Release

Double album of Jarrett at the Trinity Organ at Ottobeuren Abbey, West Germany. Pure, spacious and overflowing sound/composition. Our selections are the least experimental. In the Spheres, Jarrett moves into toneworlds never before explored on pipe organs.

RALPH VAUGHAN WILLIAMS: MASS IN G MINOR

Kings College Choir, Cambridge/The English Chamber Orchestra/David Willcocks
Angel S-36590

Credo, Sanctus-Osanna I-Benedictus-Osanna II

A pure version of this lovely Mass, considered a masterpiece of contemporary English church music.

GUISEPPE VERDI: QUATTRO PEZZI SACRI

Philharmonia Orchestra and Choir/Carlo Maria Giulini
EMI/Electrola C 065-00-016

Ave Maria

An exquisite Ave Maria with the softest, floating Amen.

All art constantly aspires towards the condition of music.

Walter Pater

J. S. BACH: MASS IN B MINOR

Soloists and Orchestra of Lausanne/Michel Corboz
RCA FVL2-5715

Chorus: And was incarnate by the Holy Ghost of the Virgin Mary . . . Chorus: And was crucified also . . .

A masterpiece — in every dimension — this is the music that places Bach with the immortals. These are two choruses we play in the hushed hours of the late night; the work itself is a vast, monumental experience.

MOZART: MASS IN C MAJOR, MISSA BREVIS IN C MAJOR, AVE VERUM CORPUS

Regenburger Choir/Orchestra of Bayerischen Rundfunks/Rafael Kubelik
Deutsche Grammophon 2530 356

Ave Verum Corpus, K618

A short, beautiful moment marked with the utmost simplicity and inwardness of expression.

EVENSONG FOR ASH WEDNESDAY

The Choir of Kings College, Cambridge/David Willcocks/Roy Goodman, solo treble
Argo ZRG 5365

Allegri: Miserere (Psalm 51)

Considered so holy it was played in the Sistine Chapel only once a year for the Vatican elite until the young Mozart heard and transcribed it, this is the highest of aspirations. If you have philosophical difficulty with the words, listen to it on the level of pure sound. Roy Goodman's voice ascends to the upper reaches of the Kings College Chapel . . . and beyond. Pir Vilayat Inayat Khan says the Allegri "represents the very highest expression of music ever."

AGRUPACION CORAL DE PAMPLONO DE ESPANA

Agrupacion Coral de Pamplono
Columbia MS-6057 (out of print)

This music came to us indirectly; it's beautiful, probably contains some Victoria, but we don't have the titles. Deep, musky sound.

KOR

Mikaeli Chamber Choir
Proprius 7770 (Audiosource, 1185 Chess Dr., Foster City, CA 94404)

Erland von Koch: Hit, O Jesu, Samloms, Den Signade Dag; Verdi: Pater Noster; Geoffray: Triptyque Marial; Purcell: Thou Knowest, Lord, the Secrets of Our Hearts

A selection of the softer, gentler sacred works performed by a Swedish choral group. Purist stereo recording produces an impeccable combination.

DURUFLE: REQUIEM, OP. 9

Orchestre de l'Association des Concerts Lamoureaux/Maurice Durufle
Musical Heritage Society, MHS 1509

Lux Aeterna

A specially lovely and refined Requiem Mass by this 20th century French composer.

MADRIGALS AND MOTETS

The Budapest Madrigal Ensemble/Ferenc Szekeres
Monitor MCS 2054

Liszt: Ave Maria, O Salutaris Hostia

Deeply reverent, tender and affecting.

I have increasingly become conversant with Pythagoras' and Goethe's idea of a primordial music, not perceptible to the sensuous ear, but sounding and soaring throughout the Cosmos. Tracing it to such exalted origins, I begin to understand more deeply the essence of our art and its elemental power over the human soul. Man, being a creature of Nature and subject to the cosmic influences that inform all earthly beings, must needs have been under the sway of that music from his earliest days; his organism reverberated with its vibrations and received its rhythmic impulses.

Bruno Walter

MUSIC FOR GRACE CATHEDRAL

The Louis Magor Singers
unpublished

Arthur Stidfole: Opalescent River Scene

Part of a thoroughly excellent 1979 concert in Grace Cathedral, Opalescent River Scene is "like the light in the mist" which inspired it.

MASTERSINGERS OF THE SAN ANTONIO SYMPHONY

Mastersingers of the San Antonio Symphony

Telarc 5026

Lotti: Crucifixus II

A good selection of sacred choral pieces, sung with lusty Texan enthusiasm. There are probably more subtle versions of the Lotti, which is lovely and moving.

J.S. BACH: MAGNIFICAT IN D, CANTATA #51

Teresa Stich-Randall, Soprano; M. Andre, Trumpet/The Chamber Orchestra of the Sarre/ Karl Ristenpart
Nonesuch H-71011

Cantata #51: Recitative

Lovely, hushed section of a joyous work.

A TREASURY OF GREGORIAN CHANT VOL. II

Monks of the Abbey of St. Thomas
VOX STP516.470

Introit (Mode 4), Communion (Mode 7), Offertory (Mode 8), Alleluia (Mode 2) Communion (Mode 8)

Pure Western devotional music. This album is one of many excellent recordings available. The combination of male voices in harmony and the ambience of stone churches creates one of the most powerful spaces for the Western psyche.

RACHMANINOFF: LITURGY OF ST. JOHN CHRYSOSTOM

Chorus of the Bulgarian Radio, Sofia/Mikhil Milkov
Angel SB 3864 (2 disc)

Russian religious music with Byzantine roots, recorded in the Alexander Nevsky Cathedral in Sofia with its 9 second reverberation. Very deep.

RELATED MUSIC

PSALMS OF CONSOLATION AND HOPE

**The Choir of St. John's College, Cambridge/
George Guest**
ARGO ZRG 892
Psalm 49, Psalm 23

BRITTEN:
A CEREMONY OF CAROLS, HYMN
TO ST. CECILIA, MISSA BREVIS

Kings College Choir/David Willcocks
Seraphim S-60217
A Ceremony of Carols: VIII. (In Freezing Winter Night);
XI (Recession); I (Procession)

MOTETS OF THOMAS TALLIS

The Clerkes of Oxenford/David Wulstan
Seraphim S-60256
Spem in allium

BRAHMS: SACRED AND SECULAR
CHORAL MUSIC

**Chorus of the Gulbenkian Foundation of
Lisbon/Michel Corboz**
RCA ARL1-3350
Motet, Op 74, No. 1

DESMARETS: MYSTERES DE
NOTRE SEIGNEUR JESUS-CHRIST

**Vocal and Instrumental Ensemble of Lyon/Guy
Cornut**
Musical Heritage Society MHS 4085
Descente Du Saint-Esprit

*When the human
being sings he
lends expression
to the great wise
ways in which the
world was made.*

Rudolf Steiner

*. . . Bach, like every other lofty religious mind, belongs not to the church but
to religious humanity, and . . . any room becomes a church in which his
sacred works are performed and listened to with devotion.*

Albert Schweitzer

THE SINKING OF THE TITANIC

Gavin Bryars
Obscure No. 1

Jesus' Blood Never Failed Me Yet

A tape loop of several lines from a heartfelt hymn sung by an elderly English hobo — with strings, bass, woodwind, French horns, harp, brass, oboe, organ and vibes added gradually. Very moving. Produced by Brian Eno.

ON THE OTHER OCEAN

David Behrman
Lovely Music

On the Other Ocean

An interactive piece with Maggi Payne, flute, Arthur Stidfole, bassoon, and a microcomputer-controlled synthesizer, creating a soothing, meditative continuity.

FLYING DREAMS

Victor Spiegel
HS 798, Halpern Sounds, 620 Taylor Way, #14, Belmont, CA 94002

Flying Dreams II

First cassette album by a composer/keyboard virtuoso whose solo piano improvisations will inevitably be compared to Keith Jarrett's. (He's that good.) The listed selection is for electric piano and flute — more spacey and formless than the piano music.

2001: A SPACE ODYSSEY

Ormandy: The Philadelphia Orchestra, Bernstein: New York Philharmonic
Columbia MS-7176

Ligeti: Atmospheres; Lux Aeterna

The only real space music in the soundtrack to Stanley Kubrick's classic vision of our future in space. Mystical/mysterious.

BEYOND THE BLUE HORIZON

Lou Christie
Three Bros. THB-402 (single)

Beyond the Blue Horizon

You may think it's campy at first, but it'll have you dancing and singing along by the fourth chorus. Inspiring comic relief.

ALL I SEE IS YOU

Rabindra Danks
Takoma/Devi D-1036

Tippy Tapping

A foot-tapping satire on the joys of meditation, Dixieland style.

A FAMILY AFFAIR

The Speers
Heart Warming Records 3147

Turn Your Radio On

Whatever its original intention, this is a great anthem to turned-on radio . . . . "Get in touch with God (space fan) . . . Turn your radio on."

The whole of life in all its aspects is one single music; and the real spiritual attainment is to tune one's self to the harmony of this perfect music.

Hazrat Inayat Khan

THE WORLD IS STILL WAITING FOR THE SUNRISE

Les Paul and Mary Ford
Capitol ST-11308

Vaya con Dios

If audio tapes came in black and white, this would be one of them. Innocent.

JASON SERINUS: WHISTLER EXTRAORDINAIRE

Jason Serinus
Jason Serinus, 80 Elgin Park, No. 4, San Francisco, CA 94103 (cassette)

Virtuoso soprano whistling of classical arias and popular songs by Jason Serinus, the Voice of Woodstock in Peanuts cartoons, whose inner approach to his art is that "whistling is focused breath."

RELATED MUSIC

LA VOIX ET LA MUSIQUE DE GURDJIEFF

Gurdjieff
G.I.G. 001/2 (Harmonium)

FAIRPORT CONVENTION

Fairport Convention
SP-4185
The Lord is in This Place ... How Dreadful Is This Place

PERUVIAN WHISTLING VESSELS

Steven Halpern and Daniel K. Stat
SRI 781, Halpern Sounds, 620 Taylor Way, #14, Belmont, CA 94002

CLARA ROCKMORE: THEREMIN

Clara Rockmore, theremin; Nadia Reisenberg, piano
Delos DEL-25437

G. T. GURDJIEFF: SACRED HYMNS

Keith Jarrett
ECM 1-1174
Reading of Sacred Books

CALDARA: STABAT MATER

Robert Margouleff, Malcolm Cecil, John Atkins
Kama Sutra KSBS 2020 (out of print)
Electronic music parts only

LEDA

Linda Cohen
Poppy PYS-5702
Fantasia Inca

Your music is my world
        but only for this moment
because of the others
                we are closer

Will we be here
                travelling
As one

        We are passion
            through time
over the mountain, up

                into the sky

                to no place

I have been before

        endlessly

        At last,

        quiet

Nina Ireland

RELATED MATERIAL

There is an increasing number of books, tapes and articles on music and sound representing a variety of cosmological perspectives. This is by no means an inclusive list; rather, these are things we have personally experienced and can so recommend.

Books

These two books have been the most deeply instructive and inspiring to us and we can recommend them wholeheartedly:

Peter Michael Hamel. **Through Music to the Self.** Shambhala Publications, Inc., 1123 Spruce St., Boulder, CO 80302. This book is just essential.

The Sufi Message of Hazrat Inayat Khan, Vol. II. "The Mysticism of Sound," "Music," "The Power of the Word," "Cosmic Language." From Hunter House, Inc., Publishers, 748 E. Bonita Ave., #105, Pomona, CA 91767.

Other Books on Music

Edward B. Benjamin, Sr. **The Restful in Music.** Crescendo Publishing Co., 48-50 Melrose St., Boston, MA 02116. Extensive listing of quiet movements from Western classical compositions.

Sri Chinmoy. **God, the Supreme Musician.** Agni Press, 84-47 Parsons Rd., Jamaica, NY 11432. Thoughts and poetry from an Indian spiritual teacher.

Lionel Stebbing. **Music, Its Occult Basis and Healing Value.** New Knowledge Books, P.O. Box 9, Horsham, Sussex, RH12 2LB, England. Writings of Rudolf Steiner and his students on secular and cosmic music, music therapy and related topics.

Shirley Rabb Winston. **Music as the Bridge.** A.R.E. Press, P.O. Box 595, Virginia Beach, VA 23451. Information on music compiled from the channelings of Edgar Cayce.

Periodicals

Parabola, Myth and the Quest for Meaning. May, 1980 issue (Vol. V, No. 2) devoted to "Music, Sound, Silence." Parabola, 150 Fifth Avenue, New York, N.Y. 11202.

Tapes

Sound, a talk by Pir Vilayat Khan. Tape T9 from Sufi Order Publications, P.O. Box 5568, Lebanon Springs, NY 12114.

Iasos: Sound and the Cosmos, interview by Will Noffke. Co-Creative Productions, 2512 San Pablo Ave., Berkeley, CA 94702. In addition, Will Noffke will be publishing interviews with many musicians in the near future, including Alan Hovhaness, Hidayat Khan, Steven Halpern, Sande Hershman, Stephen Fiske and Buddy Comfort. Write for information.

Metaphysical Perspective on Iasos' Work, from Inter-Dimensional Music, P.O. Box 594, Waldo Pt., Sausalito, CA 94965.

INTER-RELATED MATERIAL

The Seth Material is a body of information dictated by an energy personality essence named Seth who speaks through Jane Roberts, a writer and trance medium in Elmira, New York. It is provocative, expansive and exuberant. Though there are as yet unpublished sessions dealing with sound, some tastes can be found in the following:

> **Seth Speaks,** pp. 248-251, 441, 439.
> **The Nature of Personal Reality,** p. 98 ff
> **The 'Unknown' Reality,** Vol. II, pp. 403, 478-483.
> **The Nature of the Psyche,** pp. 101-105.

Continuum is a studio in Los Angeles founded by Emilie Conrad-Da'oud which teaches some of the most advanced work we know in movement and sound meditation. It has opened to our awareness an entirely new category of music, which we call Cellular Wave Music. Daily classes are held in Los Angeles, and weekly or monthly workshops in the San Francisco area. Emilie Conrad-Da'oud has been instrumental in pioneer research conducted on the human aura at UCLA by Dr. Valerie Hunt. Descriptions of this work are contained in two interview tapes by Will Noffke of Co-Creative Productions: Dr. Valerie Hunt, Emilie Conrad-Da'oud, Rosalyn Bruyere; and one with Susan Harper and Michael Stearns of Continuum. Or write Continuum, 3640-1/2 Watseka Ave., Los Angeles, CA 90034. (This is an address for information only; classes are not held here.)

The Silent Pulse by George Leonard (Bantam Books, 1980) is a wonderful book, beautifully written, on the rhythmic interrelationships of our world, with examples from music and aikido to physics and life experience, and the postulate that there is a state of perfect rhythm, which some would call a state of grace, which we can learn to find and enter.

Rhythms of Vision, an important book by Lawrence Blair (Warner Books, 1975), not only contains some tantalizing information on sound, but is, overall, an exciting journey through the interconnection points of ancient science and esoterism with modern science and Aquarian philosophy.

The New Dimensions Tape Catalogue is a listing of 600 audio cassettes compiled from spontaneous radio conversations broadcast over the past 8 years in the San Francisco Bay Area and now, via public radio satellite, in 70 cities across the country. Categories include Holistic Health and Wellness; Shamans, Sorcerers, Wizards and Other Wonders; Evolutionary Economics; The Psychic Realm; Right Living; Self Help; Visionary Futures; Practical Philosophy. Write for a free catalogue: New Dimensions Radio, Dept. MC, 267 States St., San Francisco, CA 94114.

Eurock is a high integrity magazine published and lovingly evolved over the last 7 years by Archie Patterson. He covers the European electronic, new music, and avant garde art/music scene like no one else, and was our original connection to artists like Peter Michael Hamel, Klaus Schulze, Popol Vuh, Ashra and many others. Last year he launched **Eurock Distribution** which should grow into a major supply point for European and Japanese new music. Write for subscription information and an up-to-date catalogue of mail order records and tapes. **Eurock,** P.O. Box 4181, Torrance, CA 90510.

Emmett E. Miller, M.D. has produced some of the finest guided imagery, stress-reduction and self-improvement tapes we've heard, many with original music by such artists as Georgia Kelly, Rafiel and Steven Halpern. For information, write Emmett E. Miller, M.D., 945 Evelyn St., Menlo Park, CA 94025.

The New Age Music Network is an organization of musicians and sound and business professionals interested in facilitating the emergence of "new age music" in the world. Write The New Age Music Network, P.O. Box 9416, San Rafael, CA 94902 for a sample newsletter.

BAY AREA RETAIL SOURCES

San Francisco

Aeon Books
2199 Market St.
San Francisco, CA 94114
415/621-2040

Amron Psychic World
1863 Union St.
San Francisco, CA 94123
415/567-1723

Atlantis Metaphysical Bookshop
584 O'Farrell St.
San Francisco, CA 94102
415/775-9250

Rooks & Becords
2222 Polk St.
San Francisco, CA 94109
415/771-7909

Star Magic
4026 1/2 24th St.
San Francisco, CA 94114
415/641-8626

East Bay

Earthsign Books
2510 San Pablo Ave.
Berkeley, CA 94702
415/548-2186

Lewin's Metaphysical Books
2644 Ashby Ave.
Berkeley, CA 94705
415/843-9152

Rather Ripped Records
4266 Broadway
Oakland, CA 94611
415/547-6701

Shambhala Booksellers
2482 Telegraph Ave.
Berkeley, CA 94704
415/848-8443

Sunrise Metaphysical Books
3054 Telegraph Ave.
Berkeley, CA 94705
415/841-6372

Marin

Paper Ships
69 Tamal Vista Blvd.
Corte Madera, CA 94925
415/924-4212

Paper Ships
79 Center Blvd.
San Anselmo, CA 94960
415/457-5990

Sonoma

Metaphysical Center
105 Montgomery Dr.
Santa Rosa, CA 95404
707/546-8810

Peninsula

East-West Book Shop
1170 El Camino Real
Menlo Park, CA 94025
415/325-5709

Minerva Books
1027 Alma
Palo Alto, CA 94301
415/326-2006

Palo Alto Health Food Store
463 University Ave.
Palo Alto, CA 94301
415/328-5810

Plowshare
162 University Ave.
Palo Alto, CA 94301
415/321-4748

*Imagine yourselves out there in the universe. From all the heavenly bodies it
is singing, speaking as it sings, singing as it speaks, and all your perception
is a listening to this speech which is song, the singing speech of the Cosmos.
Picture it as vividly as you can. The spheres of the fixed stars more at rest;
behind it the wandering planets. And whenever a planet in its course passes a
constellation of the fixed stars, there bursts forth, not one single note, but a
whole world of music. Then as the planet passes on . . . from one
constellation to another, a different world of sound rings out. Behind there
follows, let us say, another planet . . . passing through the constellation . . .
It causes a different world of sound to ring forth. Thus we have in the heavens
of the fixed stars a wondrous Cosmic instrument of Music, while from the
planets behind it the planetary Spirits are playing upon this instrument.*

Rudolf Steiner

MAIL ORDER SOURCES

Music from the Hearts of Space
P.O. Box 31321
San Francisco, CA 94131

Fortuna
11 Kavon
Novato, CA 94947

Celestial Harmonies
605 Ridgefield Rd.
Wilton, CT 06897

Source
1307 Buena Vista
Pacific Grove, CA 93950

Greenworld Records Limited
23703 Madison St.
Torrance, CA 90505

Rather Ripped Records
4266 Broadway
Oakland, CA 94611

Passport Imports
3146 E. Burnside
Portland, OR 97214

Omega Music
Box 569
Lebanon Springs, NY 12114

The Orion Foundation
Box 757
Puunene, Maui, Hawaii 96784

Musical Heritage Society
14 Park Road
Tinton Falls, NJ 07724

While many of the records and tapes listed in this guide may be found in or ordered through conventional record retailers, many others are only available through specialized stores or by mail.

Simultaneous with the publication of this Guide, **Music from the Hearts of Space** is launching its own mail order record and tape sales service. While we sincerely hope that you will order some of your music from us (it makes it all possible, friends), our initial catalogue is limited to only 33 albums we consider top quality and "essential."

For your convenience we include here a number of other mail order sources, some with very extensive catalogues. Perhaps at some point in our lifetimes direct electronic distribution via satellite, cable, or who-knows-what will make all these low-ecology packages of plastic unnecessary. But for now, intelligent use of catalogues is the most efficient way to access unusual music.

INDEX

COLOPHON

This book was produced co-creatively with much care by many people:

The listings were prepared on Dan Dugan's microcomputersystem using DIMS (Dan's Information Management System) and WordStar.

These computerized listings were converted and additional copy was typeset on VIP by Bob Sibley of Abracadabra, San Francisco. The text typeface is ITC Eras, the quotes are ITC Benguiat italic, and headlines are Friz Quadrata.

The cover calligraphy was created by William Stewart of San Francisco.

Book design and art direction was by Janaia Marisolle of Chrysalis of Arts, Palo Alto, with production assistance by John Haynes.

The book production was done by UCSC Extension graphics students Carolyn Gong- Guy, Susan Hall, Bev. Kelly, Sheri Mak, Barbara Moon, Trudi Reinhard, Terry Schnitz, Lynne Stevens, Jim Strand, Gail Tremblay, Marva Warnock, Beverly Whitaker and Claire Zurak.

The book was proofed by Ursula Krainock and Rosalind McRoskey.

The cover illustration star dome, inspired by a 13th- century Islamic temple design, was computer-generated by John Warnock of Xerox PARC, and then handworked in pen and airbrush by Janaia Marisolle.

Inside illustrations were created by David Porrazzo (page 54) and Janaia Marisolle (frontispiece and 90).

Photographs on pages 21, 26, 87 and 93 are by Steven Mangold of Los Gatos.

Poem on page 91 by Nina Ireland.

This edition of 1,000 was printed by Graphius NV in Gent, Belgium.

Published by Colpa Press and Amaya Productions, 2025.

ISBN 978-1-7379905-1-2

CAN'T UNDERSTAND CALIFORNS
THEY TALK TOO SLOW

AFTERWORD

Three times I have 'gone' to a place that I cannot find words to describe accurately. . . . To me, it was a place or condition of pure peace, yet exquisite emotion. It was as if you were floating in warm soft clouds where there is no up or down, where nothing exists as a separate piece of matter. The warmth is not merely around you, it is of you and through you. Your perception is dazzled and overwhelmed by the Perfect Environment.

The cloud in which you float is swept by rays of light in shapes and hues that are constantly changing, and each is good as you bathe in them as they pass over you. Ruby-red rays of light, or something beyond what we know as light, because no light ever **felt** this meaningful. All the colors of the spectrum come and go constantly, never harshly, and each brings a different soothing or restful happiness. It is as if you are within and a part of the clouds surrounding an eternally glowing sunset, and with every changing pattern of living color, you also change. You respond and drink into you the eternity of the blues, yellows, greens, and reds, and the complexities of the intermediates. All here is familiar to you. This is where you belong. This is Home.

As you move slowly and effortlessly through the cloud, there is music around you. It is not something of which you become aware. It is there all the time, and you vibrate in harmony with the Music. Again, this is more than the music you knew back there. It is only those harmonies, the delicate and dynamic melodic passages, the multivoiced counterpoint, the poignant overtones—it is only those that have evoked in you the deep, incoherent emotion back there. The mundane is missing. Choirs of human-sounding voices echo in wordless song. Infinite patterns of strings in all shades of subtle harmony interweave in cyclical yet developing themes, and you resonate with them. There is no source from which the Music comes. It is there, all around you, in you, you are a part of it, and it is you.

It is the purity of a truth of which you have had only a glimpse. This is the feast, and the tiny tidbits you tasted before, back there, had made you hope for the existence of the Whole. The nameless emotion, longing, nostalgia, sense of destiny that you felt back there when you stared at the cloud-layered sunset in Hawaii, when you stood quietly among the tall, waving trees in the silent forest, when a musical selection, passage, or song recalled memories of the past or brought forth a longing for which there was no associated memory, when you longed for the place where you belonged, whether city, town, country, nation, or family—these are now fulfilled. You are Home. You are where you belong. Where you always should have been.

Robert A. Monroe

Robert A. Monroe. **Journeys Out of the Body,** pp. 123, 121. Garden City, New York: Anchor Press, 1977.

Rising in space

    for its ownsake

free and

open

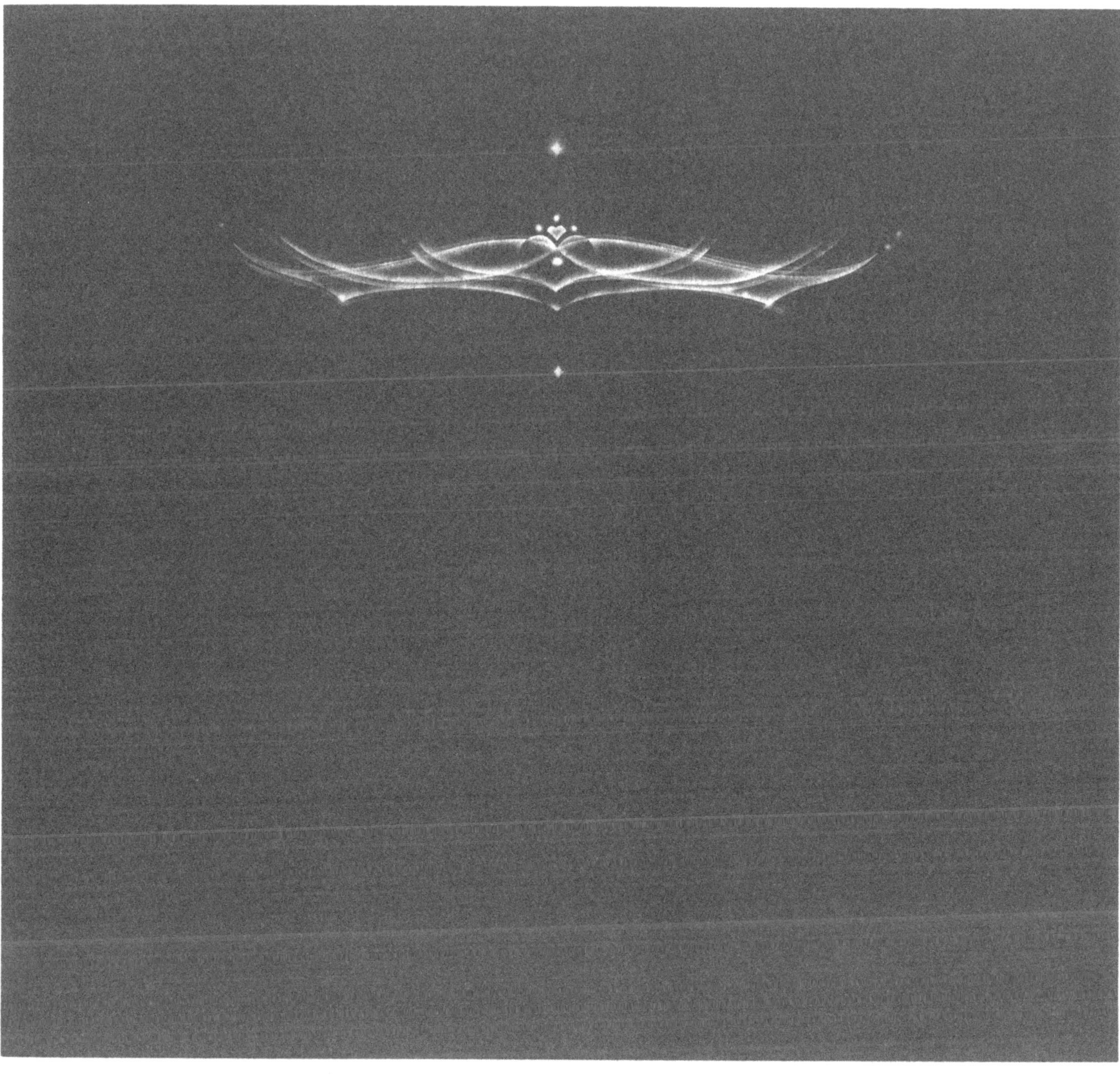